Communications
in Computer and Information Science   787

Commenced Publication in 2007
Founding and Former Series Editors:
Alfredo Cuzzocrea, Xiaoyong Du, Orhun Kara, Ting Liu, Dominik Ślęzak,
and Xiaokang Yang

More information about this series at http://www.springer.com/series/7899

Derek F. Wong · Deyi Xiong (Eds.)

Machine Translation

13th China Workshop, CWMT 2017
Dalian, China, September 27–29, 2017
Revised Selected Papers

 Springer

Editors
Derek F. Wong
University of Macau
Macau SAR
China

Deyi Xiong
Soochow University
Suzhou
China

ISSN 1865-0929 ISSN 1865-0937 (electronic)
Communications in Computer and Information Science
ISBN 978-981-10-7133-1 ISBN 978-981-10-7134-8 (eBook)
https://doi.org/10.1007/978-981-10-7134-8

Library of Congress Control Number: 2017959722

This Springer imprint is published by Springer Nature
The registered company is Springer Nature Singapore Pte Ltd.
The registered company address is: 152 Beach Road, #21-01/04 Gateway East, Singapore 189721, Singapore

Preface

The China Workshop on Machine Translation (CWMT) brings together researchers and practitioners in the area of machine translation, providing a forum for those in academia and industry to exchange and promote the latest development in methodologies, resources, projects, and products that can be shared among all the researchers and practitioners, with a special emphasis on the language in China. The CWMT forums have been successfully held in Xiamen (2005, 2011), Beijing (2006, 2008, 2010), Harbin (2007), Nanjing (2009), Xian (2012), Kunming (2013), Macau (2014), Hefei (2015), and Urumqi (2016), featuring a variety of activities, including an Open Source Systems Development (2006), two Strategic Meetings (2010, 2012) and six Machine Translation Evaluations (2007, 2008, 2009, 2011, 2013, 2015). These activities have made a substantial impact on advancing the research and development of machine translation. The workshop has been a highly productive forum for the progress of this area and considered as a leading and an important academic event in the natural language processing field in China.

This year, the 13th CWMT was held in Dalian, China, at the Dalian University of Technology. This workshop continued being the most important academic event dedicated to machine translation and its theoretical and technological advances. It hosted the 7th Machine Translation Evaluation Campaign and the Second Machine Translation Forum (MT Forum), featured a keynote speech delivered by Mike Schuster (Google), and four invited talks delivered by Jean Senellart (SYSTRAN), Weihua Luo (Alibaba), Zhongjun He (Baidu), and Feifei Zhai (Sogou), exploring the cutting-edge technologies in machine translation and the best practices in its applications.

A total of 26 submissions were received for the main meeting. All the papers were carefully reviewed in a double-blind manner and each paper was evaluated by at least three members of an international scientific committee (Program Committee). From the submissions, the 16 best papers were accepted to be presented at this workshop, of which 11 were English papers. These papers address all aspects of machine translation, including preprocessing, neural machine translation models, hybrid model, evaluation method, and post-editing, with a focus on the translation of Chinese from/to English and minority languages.

We would like to express our thanks to every person and institution involved in the organization of this workshop, especially the members of the Program Committee, the Machine Translation Evaluation campaign, the MT forum, the invited speakers, the local organization team, the sponsors, and the organizations that supported and promoted the event. Last but not least, we greatly appreciate Springer for publishing the proceedings.

September 2017

Derek F. Wong
Deyi Xiong

Organization

Honorary Chairs

Chengqing Zong   Institute of Automation, Chinese Academy of Sciences, China

Le Sun   Institute of Software, Chinese Academy of Sciences, China

Tiejun Zhao   Harbin Institute of Technology, China

Xiaodong Shi   Xiamen University, China

Conference Chair

Qun Liu   Dublin City University, Ireland
Institute of Computing Technology, Chinese Academy of Sciences, China

Program Co-chairs

Derek F. Wong   University of Macau, Macau SAR, China

Deyi Xiong   Soochow University, China

MT Evaluation Chair

Shujian Huang   Nanjing University, China

Machine Translation Forum Chairs

Jingbo Zhu   Northeastern University, China

Yongpeng Wei   Lingosail, China

Program Committee

António Branco   University of Lisbon, Portugal
Hailong Cao   Harbin Institute of Technology, China
Lidia S. Chao   University of Macau, Macau SAR, China
Yidong Chen   Xiamen University, China
Yufeng Chen   Beijing Jiaotong University, China
Xiangyu Duan   Soochow University, China
Chong Feng   Beijing Institute of Technology, China
Qin Gao   Google, USA
Yuhang Guo   Beijing Institute of Technology, China
Yanqing He   Institute of Scientific and Technical Information of China, China

Zhongjun He	Baidu, China
Shujian Huang	Nanjing University, China
Wenbin Jiang	Institute of Computing Technology, Chinese Academy of Sciences, China
Hongfei Jiang	Dinfo Co. Ltd., China
Jianfeng Li	Iflytek Co. Ltd., China
Junhui Li	Soochow University, China
Lemao Liu	National Institute of Information and Communications Technology, Japan
Shujie Liu	Microsoft Research Asia, China
Yang Liu	Tsinghua University, China
Weihua Luo	Alibaba International Business Operations, China
Cunli Mao	Kunming University of Science and Technology, China
Fandong Meng	Tencent, China
Haitao Mi	Ant Financial, China
Mino Hideya	National Institute of Information and Communications Technology, Japan
Jinsong Su	Xiamen University, China
Zhaopeng Tu	Tencent AI Lab, China
Mingxuan Wang	Tencent, China
Ling Wang	Google Deepmind, USA
Wei Wang	Google, USA
Andy Way	ADAPT Centre, Dublin City University, Ireland
Tong Xiao	Northeastern University, China
Mo Yu	IBM Watson, USA
Yating Yang	Xinjiang Technical Institute of Physics and Chemistry, Chinese Academy of Sciences, China
Xiaojun Zhang	University of Stirling, UK
Conghui Zhu	Harbin Institute of Technology, China
Hao Zhang	Google, USA
Jiajun Zhang	Institute of Automation, Chinese Academy of Sciences, China
Qiuye Zhao	Institute of Computing Technology, Chinese Academy of Sciences, China
Yu Zhou	Institute of Automation, Chinese Academy of Sciences, China
Yun Zhu	Beijing Normal University, China

Local Organization Chair

Degen Huang	Dalian University of Technology, China

Local Organizing Committee

Lishuang Li	Dalian University of Technology, China
Jingxiang Cao	Dalian University of Technology, China

Organizer

Chinese Information Processing Society of China

Co-organizer

Dalian University of Technology

Sponsors

Platinum Sponsors

Global Tone Communication Technology Co., Ltd.

Tencent Technology Co., Ltd.

Systran International Co., Ltd.

Beijing Atman Technology Co., Ltd.

ATMAN

Gold Sponsors

Beijing Sogou Technology Development Co., Ltd.

Beijing Lingosail Tech Co., Ltd.

Shenyang YaTrans Network Technology Co., Ltd.

Silver Sponsor

Guangxi Daring E-Commerce Services Co., Ltd.

Contents

Neural Machine Translation with Phrasal Attention

Yachao Li[1,2]([⊠]), Deyi Xiong[1], and Min Zhang[1]

[1] School of Computer Science and Technology,
Soochow University, Suzhou 215000, China
liyc7711@gmail.com, {dyxiong,minzhang}@suda.edu.cn
[2] Key laboratory of National Language Intelligent Processing,
Northwest Minzu University, Lanzhou 730030, China

Abstract. Attention-based neural machine translation (NMT) employs an attention network to capture structural correspondences between the source and target language at the word level. Unfortunately, alignments between source and target equivalents are complicated, which makes word-level attention not adequate to model these relations (e.g., alignments between a source idiom and its target translation). In order to handle this issue, we propose a phrase-level attention mechanism to complement the word-level attention network in this paper. The proposed phrasal attention framework is simple yet effective, keeping the strength of phrase-based statistical machine translation (SMT) on the source side. Experiments on Chinese-to-English translation task demonstrate that the proposed method is able to statistically improve word-level attention-based NMT.

Keywords: Neural machine translation · Attention mechaism · Recurrent neural network · Gated recurrent unit

1 Introduction

Neural machine translation, a recently proposed framework for machine translation based on sequence-to-sequence models, has gradually surpassed the state-of-the-art of statistical machine translation (SMT) over various language pairs [1–3]. In the standard Encoder-Decoder [2], a recurrent neural network (RNN) encoder, is used to encode a source sentence, and a second RNN, known as a decoder is used to predict words in the target language one by one. The vanilla NMT model has been extended with an attention mechanism [4], which is designed to predict the soft alignment between the source language and the target language. The attention-based NMT have achieved state-of-the-art results over several language pairs [8]. Most NMT models rely on word-level information, but words may not be the best candidates as basic translation units. For example, the Chinese word "XinHuaShe" is aligned to the English words "Xinhua News Agency". In this case, it is better to consider the English word sequence "Xinhua

© Springer Nature Singapore Pte Ltd. 2017
D.F. Wong and D. Xiong (Eds.): CWMT 2017, CCIS 787, pp. 1–8, 2017.
https://doi.org/10.1007/978-981-10-7134-8_1

News Agency" as the appropriate translation unit. However, the existing NMT models do not allow us to perform such kind of alignment.

To avoid such deficiency of word-level sequence-to-sequence models, the structural information from word-based alignment models has been incorporated into the attention-based NMT models [5,6]. In order to enhance the attention mechanism [9] proposed a supervised attention for NMT that is supervised by statistical alignment models. The work of [7] proposed a tree-to-sequence attention-based NMT that enables the decoder to align a translated word with phrases as well as words of the source language sentence.

Partially inspired by the works above, we incorporate phrasal attention into attention-based NMT. The idea behind is enabling the NMT model to consider both word- and phrase-level information during decoding simultaneously. Embeddings of source phrases are automatically learned, upon which the phrasal attention network is built to capture m-to-1 correspondence relations during translation. We further propose a gating mechanism to dynamically control the ratios at which word and phrase contexts contribute to the generation of target words.

Experiments on Chinese to English translation datasets show that the proposed approach significantly improves translation quality and it can obviously improve the word alignment quality.

2   Neural Machine Translation with Phrasal Attention

In this section, we give a brief introduction to vanilla neural machine translation and the word-level attention-based NMT. We then explain the issue of word alignments with the latter NMT, and propose a novel model to alleviate such deficiency.

2.1   Neural Machine Translation

In the vanilla Encoder-Decoder framework [2], an encoder reads a source language sentence, a sequence of words $\mathbf{x} = (x_1, \ldots, x_I)$, and encodes it into a vector $\mathbf{c}$. Then, the decoder generates a target language sentence word by word. It defines a probability for each generated target word given the context vector c and all the previously generated words $(y_1, \ldots, y_{t-1})$. The probability of the generated target sentence can then be calculated as follows:

$$p(\mathbf{y}) = \prod_{t=1}^{T} p(y_t \mid y_1, \ldots, y_{t-1}, \mathbf{c}) \tag{1}$$

$$p(y_t \mid y_1, \ldots, y_{t-1}, \mathbf{c}) = g(y_{t-1}, s_t, \mathbf{c}) \tag{2}$$

$$s_t = f(s_{t-1}, y_{t-1}, \mathbf{c}) \tag{3}$$

where g is a nonlinear function, $\mathbf{y} = (y_1, \ldots, y_T)$, s_t is the hidden state of the decoder. $\mathbf{c}$ is the context vector, modeled as:

$$\mathbf{c} = q(h_1, \ldots, h_I) \tag{4}$$

$$h_i = f(x_i, h_{i-1}) \tag{5}$$

where q and f are nonlinear functions, h_i is the i-th hidden state of the encoder, which is considered to be an encoding corresponding to x_i.

The whole model is jointly trained to maximize the conditional log-likelihood of the training data:

$$L(\theta) = \max_\theta \frac{1}{N} \sum_{n=1}^{N} logp_\theta(y_n \mid x_n) \tag{6}$$

where θ is a set of all parameters, each (x_n, y_n) is a pair (source language sentence, target language sentence) from the training set.

In attention-based NMT [4], the context vector is generated dynamically at each time step in decoding. In the new model architecture, the conditional probability in Eq. (2) is then computed by:

$$p(y_t \mid y_1, \ldots, y_{t-1}, \mathbf{x}) = g(y_{t-1}, s_t, c_t) \tag{7}$$

$$s_t = f(s_{t-1}, y_{t-1}, c_t) \tag{8}$$

where s_t is t-th hidden unit of the decoder.

The context vector c_t is calculated as the summation vector weighted by a_{ti}:

$$c_t = \sum_{i=1}^{I} a_{ti} h_i \tag{9}$$

where a_{ti} is the weight of h_i, defined as

$$a_{ti} = \frac{exp(e_{ti})}{\sum_{k=1}^{I} exp(e_{tk})} \tag{10}$$

where $e_{ti} = a(s_{t-1}, h_i)$ is an alignment model, measuring the degree of matching between the i-th source hidden unit h_i and the t-th target hidden unit s_t.

According to the description above, the attention-based NMT integrates more word-level source language information into the decoding process, thus significantly improves the translation performance [4,8].

2.2 Phrasal Attention Model

Most existing NMT models treat words as the units for translation and neglect the correspondence relations between multi-word terms of the source language and single word in the target language. We therefore propose a novel phrase-based encoder to explicitly incorporate the phrasal information into the attention-based NMT model. The overall diagram of our proposed model is displayed in Fig. 1.

Formally, given a source language sentence $\mathbf{x} = (x_1, \ldots, x_I)$, phrases corresponding to the given sentence are $\mathbf{p} = (p_1, \ldots, p_K)$, $p_k \in \mathbf{x}$, $p_k =$

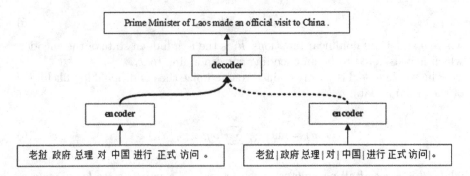

Fig. 1. The overall diagram for neural machine translation with phrasal attention. We incorporate a phrasal encoder into the standard attention-based NMT (denoted by the dotted line), the proposed model has two encoders and one decoder. During decoding, it can capture the word-level information and phrase-level information at the same time. In the phrasal encoder, the symbol | denote the phrase segmentation mark.

$(x_m, \ldots, x_n)$, $m \geq 0, n \leq I$, which are subject to the following constraints: $p_1 \cup p_2 \cup, \ldots, \cup p_K = \mathbf{x}$. A phrase is defined as a sequence of words that appear consecutively in the source language sentence. Notice that there are no overlapping parts between the phrases of a sentence.

The phrase encoder is implemented as a bi-directional recurrent neural network with gated recurrent unit. The forward RNN reads an input phrase, and then encodes the input into a sequence of forward hidden states $(\overrightarrow{hp_m}, \ldots, \overrightarrow{hp_n})$. The backward RNN reads the phrase in the reverse order (from hp_n to hp_m), and encodes the input into backword hidden states $(\overleftarrow{hp_m}, \ldots, \overleftarrow{hp_n})$. We obtain an annotation for each phrase P_k by concatenating the forward hidden state $\overrightarrow{hp}$ and the backward one $\overleftarrow{hp}$, resulting in $h'_k = [\overrightarrow{hp}; \overleftarrow{hp}]$. Therefore, $\mathbf{h}' = (h'_1, \ldots, h'_K)$, where h'_k denotes the k-th hidden state of the phrase-based encoder, which is considered as the representation of a source language phrase.

Similar to word-level attention-based NMT, the context vector $\mathbf{c}'$ of the proposed phrasal attention is defined as:

$$c'_t = \sum_{k=1}^{K} a'_{tk} h'_k \tag{11}$$

a'_{tk} is the weight of h'_k, defined as:

$$a'_{tk} = \frac{exp(e'_{tk})}{\sum_{j=1}^{K} exp(e'_{tj})} \tag{12}$$

$e'_{tk} = a(s_{t-1}, h'_k)$ is the alignment model, measuring the degree of matching between the k-th source hidden unit h'_k and the t-th target hidden unit s_t.

2.3   Integrating Phrasal Attention into NMT

We implemented two attention networks, namely word- and phrase-level attention. Our proposed model computes attention to sequential hidden units and phrase hidden units at the same time. The new context vector **ctx** is composed of the word-level context vector c_t in Eq. (9) and phrase-level context vectors c'_t in Eq. (11), defined as:

$$ctx_t = \alpha_t c_t + (1 - \alpha_t)c'_t \tag{13}$$

$$\alpha_t = g_{gate}(y_{t-1}, c'_t, c_t) \tag{14}$$

where $g_{gate}(.)$ is a sigmoid function.

Thus the conditional probability in Eq. (6) is then calculated as:

$$p(y_t \mid y_1, \ldots, y_{t-1}, \mathbf{x}) = g(y_{t-1}, s_t, ctx_t) \tag{15}$$

$$s_t = f(s_{t-1}, y_{t-1}, ctx_t) \tag{16}$$

Our proposed fusion method is simple yet effective. In the decoding phase, word-level attention information and phrase-level attention information can be taken into account simultaneously. Both of them can have an impact on the generation of target words. We use gating mechanism to dynamically control the ratios that the word- and phrase-level contexts contribute to the generation of target words. In this way, we can enhance the m-to-1 correspondence relations.

3   Experiments

3.1   Settings

We carry out experiments on Chinese-English translation. The training dataset consists of 1.25M sentence pairs extracted from LDC corpora, with 27.9M Chinese words and 34.5M English words respectively. The NIST 2002 (MT02) is chosen as the development set, and the NIST 2003 (MT03), and 2005 (MT05) datasets are used as our test sets. We use the case-insensitive 4-gram NIST BLEU score for evaluation. For efficient training of the neural machine translation, we limit the source and target vocabularies to the most frequent 30K words in Chinese and English, covering approximately 97.7 and 99.3% of the data in the two languages respectively. All out of vocabulary words are mapped to a special token *UNK*.

3.2   Training Details

We train each model with sentences of length up to 50 words in the training data. The word embedding dimension is 620. The phrase embedding dimension is 620. The size of a hidden layer is 1000. The beam size for decoding is 10. We choose adadelta [12] to optimize model parameters in training with the mini-batch size of 80. We segment each source language sentence into a sequence of proper phrases by the Max-Match algorithm, where all the phrases are no more than 9 words.

Table 1. Experimental results for different systems. The strong baseline, denoted RNNSearch, is our in-house attention-based NMT system. Ours is the proposed model.

System	MT02	MT03	MT05	AVE.
Moses	33.41	31.61	33.48	32.83
RNNSearch	37.38	35.00	34.32	35.57
Ours	**38.22**	**36.70**	**35.18**	**36.70**

Table 2. Effect of phrasal attention and gating mechanism. $+\alpha = 0$ is our model with fixed gate value 0, indicates the weight of phrasal attention is 0; $+\alpha = 0.3$ indicates our model with fixed gate value 0.3, which ignore flexible gating mechanism; +random indicates the phrases of a source sentence is generated randomly.

System	MT02	MT03	MT05	AVE.
Ours	**38.22**	**36.70**	**35.18**	**36.70**
$+\alpha = 0$	32.56	31.64	29.77	31.32
$+\alpha = 0.3$	35.32	34.12	33.01	34.15
+random	35.38	34.51	32.78	34.22

Table 3. Evaluation of alignment quality. The lower the score, the better the alignment quality.

System	AER
RNNSearch	47.6
Ours	**46.7**

We compare our method with two state-of-the-art models of SMT and NMT

- Moses: an open source phrased-based SMT system with default configuration and a 4-gram language model trained on the target portion of the training data.
- RNNSearch: our in-house attention-based NMT system [4] with slight changes taken from dl4mt tutorial. RNNSearch uses the gated recurrent unit (GRU) recently proposed by [2] as the activation function, and improves the attention mechanism by feeding the lastly generated word.

3.3 Main Results

The results in Table 1 show that the proposed method outperforms the baseline by 1.13 BLEU points on average. Our system is enhanced with phrasal attention over the baseline model, and there are no overlaps between source language phrases. Our model achieves significant improvement over the strong baseline model on the MT03 and MT05 by 1.7 BLEU points and 0.86 BLEU points respectively.

We performed additional experiments to further demonstrate the effectiveness of the proposed method, especially on phrasal attention and gating mechanism. We carry out the following three tests. First, we set a fixed gate value
0 for our model to block the information from phrase-level attention. We set
fixed gate values 0.3 for our model to change the gating mechanism to a fixed
mixture. During decoding, the phrases corresponding to a test sentence were
chosen from training data randomly, and the pseudo phrases were submitted to
the phrase-based encoder. From Table 2, we can observe that:

(1) Without phrasal attention, the experimental results of our proposed model
    severely drop. This indicates that phrasal attention is essential for our model.
(2) Without a flexible gating mechanism, the method proposed in this paper is
    severely degenerated on all test sets (-2.55 BLUE points for $\alpha = 0.3$). This
    shows that the gating mechanism plays an important role in our model.
(3) From the experimental results in Table 2, we can conclude that the proposed
    model generates wrong translations and has a significant decrease in perfor-
    mance (-2.48 BLEU points), which demonstrates that the quality of phrases
    is also very important for neural machine translation with phrasal attention.

3.4 Analysis on Word Alignment

We conjecture that our model with phrasal attention is also beneficial for alignment due to its capability of capturing phrase information in the phrase encoder.
To test this hypothesis, we carry out experiments of the word alignment task
on the manually-align dataset as in [10], which contains 900 manually aligned
Chinese-English sentence pairs. To evaluate alignment performance, we report
the alignment error rate (AER) [11] in Table 3.

Table 3 shows the overall alignment results on the word alignment task. From
Table 3, we can see that our proposed model significantly reduces the AER by
maintaining a phrasal attention during decoding.

4   Conclusion

In this paper, we investigated how phrase information of the source language
can be used to improve neural machine translation. We take the phrases of a
source sentence into account and build a phrase-based encoder. The attention
mechanism allows the proposed model to use not only the word-level information
but also the phrase-level information. We test the method on the task of Chinese
to English translation. The experimental results have proved the effectiveness of
our method.

Acknowledgements. This work was supported by National Natural Science Foundation of China (Grant Nos. 61525205, 61432013, 61403269), the Fundamental Research
Funds for the Central Universities of Northwest MinZu University (Grand Nos.
31920170154, 31920170153) and the Scientific Research Project of Universities in Gansu
(2016B-007).

References

1. Kalchbrenner, N., Blunsom, P.: Recurrent continuous translation models. In: Proceedings of 2013 Conference on Empirical Methods in Natural Language Processing (EMNLP 2013), pp. 1700–1709. ACL, Washington (2013)
2. Cho, K., Bahdanau, D., Bougares, F., et al.: Recurrent continuous translation models. In: Proceedings of 2014 Conference on Empirical Methods in Natural Language Processing (EMNLP 2014), pp. 1724–1734. ACL, Doha (2014)
3. Sutskever, I., Vinyals, O., Le, Q.V.: Sequence to sequence learning with neural networks. In: Advances in Neural Information Processing Systems, pp. 1724–1734. NIPS (2014)
4. Bahdanau, D., Cho, K., Bengio, Y.: Neural machine translation by jointly learning to align and translate. In: ICLR (2014)
5. Feng, S., Liu, S., Li, M., et al.: Implicit distortion and fertility models for attention-based encoder-decoder NMT model (2016). http://arxiv.org/abs/1601.03317
6. Cohn, T., Hoang, C.D.V., Vymolova, E., et al.: Incorporating structural alignment biases into an attentional neural translation model. In: NAACL 2016, pp. 3093–3102. ACL, San Diego (2016)
7. Eriguchi, A., Hashimoto, K., Tsuruoka, Y.: Tree-to-sequence attentional neural machine translation. In: ACL 2016, pp. 823–833. ACL, Berlin (2016)
8. Luong, M.-T., Pham, H., Manning, C.D.: Effective approaches to attention-based neural machine translation. In: EMNLP 2015, pp. 1412–1421. ACL, Lisbon (2015)
9. Liu, L., Utiyama, M., Finch, A.M., et al.: Incorporating structural alignment biases into an attentional neural translation model. In: COLING 2016, pp. 876–885. COLING, Osaka (2016)
10. Liu, Y., Sun, M.: Contrastive unsupervised word alignment with non-local features. In: AAAI 2015, pp. 2295–2301. AAAI, Austin (2015)
11. Och, F.J., Ney, H.: A systematic comparison of various statistical alignment models. Comput. Linguist. **29**, 19–51 (2013)
12. Zeiler, M.D.: ADADELTA: An Adaptive Learning Rate Method (2013). http://arxiv.org/abs/1212.5701

Singleton Detection for Coreference Resolution via Multi-window and Multi-filter CNN

Kenan Li[1,3], Heyan Huang[1,2(✉)], Yuhang Guo[1,2], and Ping Jian[1,2]

[1] School of Computer Science and Technology, Beijing Institute of Technology,
Beijing, China
{likenan, hhy63, guoyuhang, pjian}@bit.edu.cn
[2] Beijing Engineering Research Center of High Volume Language Information
Processing and Cloud Computing Application, 5 South Zhongguancun Street,
Beijing 100081, China
[3] Beijing Advanced Innovation Center for Imaging Technology,
Capital Normal University, Beijing 100048, People's Republic of China

Abstract. Mention detection is the first and a key stage in most of coreference resolution systems. Singleton mentions are the ones which appear only once and are not mentioned in the following texts. Singleton mentions always affect the performance of coreference resolution systems. To remove the singleton ones from the automatically predicted mentions, we propose a novel singleton detection method based on multi-window and multi-filter convolutional neural network (MMCNN). The MMCNN model can detect singleton mentions with less use of hand-designed features and more sentence information. Experiments show that our system outperforms all the existing singleton detection systems.

Keywords: Singleton detection · Coreference resolution · Convolutional neural network

1 Introduction

In recent years, we have seen some successful attempts which use coreference information to improve machine translation. Some works [1–3] performed coreference resolution on the source side to extract the coreference information of pronoun, and used the coreference information to improve the pronoun translation. Werlen and Popescu-Belis [4] presented a proof-of-concept of a coreference-aware decoder for document-level machine translation. So, we can see that the effect of coreference resolution is being found in machine translation. But existing coreference resolution systems are not performing very well. In this paper, we focus on the study of coreference resolution.

Coreference resolution that involves identification and clustering of noun phrase mentions that refer to the same real-world entity, and existing coreference systems usually consider a pipelined system, which has two steps: detecting all mentions in a text and clustering mentions into coreference chains. After the mention detection step, coreference resolution is performed on those predicted mentions. The predicted mentions can be split into three categories by their status in the gold standard: singleton

© Springer Nature Singapore Pte Ltd. 2017
D.F. Wong and D. Xiong (Eds.): CWMT 2017, CCIS 787, pp. 9–19, 2017.
https://doi.org/10.1007/978-981-10-7134-8_2

(mentioned just once and isn't included in gold mentions), mention starting a new entity with at least two mentions, and anaphora. Here is an example:

(1) Opening *[the street gate]₁*, *[they]₂* see *[two soldiers]₃* standing by *[the gate]₄* and *[they]₅* seem to be discussing *[something]₆*.

In example (1), the predicted mentions are *[the street gate]₁*, *[they]₂*, *[two soldiers]₃*, *[the gate]₄*, *[they]₅* and *[something]₆*. *[the street gate]₁* and *[the gate]₄* refer to the same entity. *[the street gate]₁* starts a new entity with at least two mentions. *[the gate]₄* is anaphoric. *[two soldiers]₃* and *[they]₅* refer to the same entity. *[two soldiers]₃* starts a new entity with at least two mentions. *[they]₅* is anaphoric. *[they]₂* and *[something]₆* are singletons. The goal of coreference resolution is to get the coreference chains {*[the street gate]₁*, *[the gate]₄*} and {*[two soldiers]₃*, *[they]₅*}. *[they]₂* and *[something]₆* will be discarded.

We have surveyed the results of some papers [6–9] in terms of gold mentions versus predicted mentions. The resluts are given in Table 1. As we can see, those systems show a significant decline in performance when running on predicted mentions. These performance gaps are worrisome, because the real goal of NLP systems is to process the raw data with no annotation. Obviously, reducing the difference of gold mentions and predicted mentions can improve coreference resolution performance. The main difference between predicted mentions and gold mentions is that singleton mentions exist only in predicted mentions but not in gold mentions. For instance, we used the rule-based mention detection algorithm from Raghunathan et al. [10] to extract mentions. We got a ratio of singleton mentions to non-singleton mentions of 1.5 to 1. There are a large number of singleton mentions taking part in the clustering process. This makes the clustering more difficult. In example (1), *[they]₅* has a high probability to be linked to singleton mention *[they]₂* in many coreference resolution systems. So, we think filtering out singleton mentions after mention detection step can improve the performance of coreference resolution.

Table 1. Performance gaps between using gold mentions and predicted mentions.

System	Dataset	Gold	Predict	Gap
Chen	CoNLL-12	70.46	59.69	10.77
Illinois-Coref	CoNLL-12	77.22	60.18	17.04
Berkeley	CoNLL-11	76.68	60.42	16.26
Berkeley	CoNLL-12	72.51	61.21	11.30
Prune-and-Score	CoNLL-12	80.26	61.56	18.70

De Marneffe et al. [11] used multiple hand-designed features to detect singleton: the morphosyntactic features, the grammatical role features and semantic environment features. The choice of features is a completely empirical process, mainly based on linguistic intuition, and trial and error. And the feature selection is task dependent, implying additional research for NLP task. Haagsma [12] proposed a singleton detection system based on word embeddings and a multi-layer perceptron (MLP). Haagsma used the mention itself, context words around the mention and other mentions rather than whole sentence as inputs. This breaks the semantic integrity of sentence, and the MLP has a poor ability of extracting feature from word embeddings. In order to minimize the use of hand-designed features and make full use of the complete semantic information contained in sentence, we explore a novel singleton detection system which uses multi-window and multi-filter convolutional neural network (MMCNN) to extract useful features from sentence. By using multi-window and multi-filter, we can extract multi-granularity level features, and extract enough information for the coarser feature. We transform words of sentence into vectors by looking up word embeddings. Then, sentence level features are learned by using a convolutional approach. We concatenate them with some additional surface features to form the final feature representation. Finally, we judge whether a mention is a singleton by a logistic regression classifier. The experimental result show that our system outperforms the two existing systems [11, 12]. To give a fuller evaluation of the coreference applications of our model, we incorporate our best model into a learning-based coreference resolution system [8].

The remainder of the paper is structured as follows. Section 2 discusses relevant works towards singleton detection. Section 3 presents the main framework and detail description of our model. Section 4 shows the specific data we use and the experimental results of our method and the compared baselines. And the conclusions are given in Sect. 5.

2 Related Work

The first step of coreference resolution system is mention extraction. In order to allow the coreference resolver to see most of the possible mentions, most systems use a high recall, low precision module to extract mention. So, there is a significant gap between gold mentions and predicted mentions. To reduce the gap, many mention filtering approaches have been tried.

Raghunathan et al. [10] used a rule-based method to remove spurious mentions such as numeric entities and pleonastic *it* pronouns. Yuan et al. [13] focused on filtering *it*, and use Decision Tree (C4.5) algorithm to classify whether *it* refers to entity based on the training data. Björkelund and Farkas [14] extracted referential and non-referential examples from the training set and train binary MaxEnt classifiers for the pronouns *it*, *we* and *you*. De Marneffe et al. [11] worked on singleton detection, and use a logistic regression classifier with both discourse-theoretically inspired semantic features and more superficial features (animacy, NE type, POS, etc.) to perform singleton detection. The state-of-the-art in mention filtering is the system described by Haagsma [12]. Haagsma proposed a system based on word embeddings and neural networks, feeding the mention itself, context words around the mention and other mentions in the context into a multi-layer perceptron to identify whether a mention is singleton.

Here, we focus on filtering the singleton mentions, and propose a new convolutional neural (CNN) network to extract sentence level features for singleton detection. In other NLP tasks, many existing works have proved that CNN could extract useful features from the word tokens to improve the performance of NLP task. Some works [15–17] used CNN to classify the relation of two target nouns in a sentence. Kim [18] reported on a series of experiments with CNN trained on top of pre-trained word vectors for sentence-level classification tasks. Iida et al. [19] used a multi-column Convolutional Neural Network (MCNN) for predicting zero anaphoric relations. An MCNN has several independent columns, each of which has its own convolutional and pooling layers.

3   Method

After mentions are predicted from raw texts, filtering out the singleton mentions can improve the performance of coreference resolution. We propose a novel singleton detection system which uses multi-window and multi-filter convolutional neural network (MMCNN) to extract sentence level features for singleton detection. Figure 1 describes the architecture of our model. First, the sentence which mention is located on is fed into a convolution-pooling layer to extract sentence level features. Then, sentence level features and additional features are directly concatenated to form the final feature representation. Finally, the logistic regression classifier computes a score to identify whether the mention is a singleton.

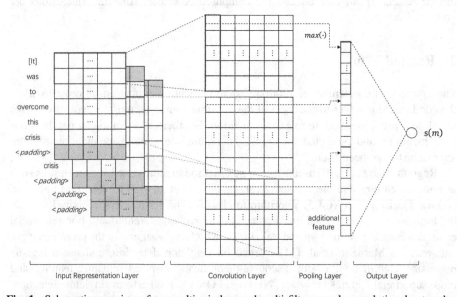

Fig. 1. Schematic overview of our multi-window and multi-filter neural convolutional network.

3.1   Input Representation

The input of the MMCNN is the sentence which mention is located on, and we want to extract context feature of mention in sentence. But the length of mention is variable, a mention can be made up of one or more words. In convolution operation, if the given mention contains many words, it's internal information could affect the context information. Peng et al. [5] proposed a coreference system which focus on mention heads rather than mentions in coreference step. This work proved that mentions had an intrinsic structure, in which mention heads carried the crucial information. So, mention head is used instead of mention as the input in this work. Given a sentence S with a target mention $\mathbf{m}$, consists of $\mathbf{n}$ words $S = \{w_1, w_2, \cdots, w_n\}$ the replace operation change S to $S^* = \{w_1, \cdots, w_{m-}, w_h, w_{m+}, \cdots, w_n\}$ where w_{m-} is the preceding word of $\mathbf{m}$, w_h is the head word of $\mathbf{m}$, w_{m+} is the following word of $\mathbf{m}$. In order to feed S^* to the MMCNN, we also need to convert S^* into real-valued vectors.

Word Embeddings. Word representations are encoded by row vectors in an embedding matrix $W^e \in \mathbb{R}^{|V| \times d^w}$, where V is a fixed-sized vocabulary, $|V|$ is the size of V, d^w is the size of the word embedding. In matrix W^e, each row $W_i^e \in \mathbb{R}^{d^w}$ corresponds to the word embedding of the i-th word in the vocabulary. We transform a word w into word embedding by:

$$r^w = look\_up(w) \tag{1}$$

where the operation $look\_up(\cdot)$ gets the index i^w of w in V, then extracts $W_{i^w}^e$ as the word embedding r^w of w.

Position Embeddings. Zeng et al. [15] proposed the use of word position embeddings (position features) to help the CNN by keeping track of how close words were to the target nouns. In this work, we use the word position embeddings (WPE) to keep track of how close the words are to the target mention $\mathbf{m}$. The WPE is derived from the relative distances of the current word to the target mention $\mathbf{m}$. For example, the relative distances of "*Opening*" and "*soldiers*" to *[the street gate]*$_1$ are -1 and 5. Each relative distance is mapped to a vector $wpe^w \in \mathbb{R}^{d^p}$, which is initialized with random numbers.

Finally, the word embedding and the position embedding of each word are concatenated to form the input for the convolutional layer, a real-valued matrix $S^e = \{emb^{w_1}, emb^{w_2}, \cdots, emb^{w_n}\}$, where $emb^{w_i} = [r^{w_i}, wpe^{w_i}] \in \mathbb{R}^{d^w + d^p}$.

3.2 Convolution and Pooling

In the next step, the matrix S^e is fed into the convolutional layer to extract higher level features. We use multi-window and multi-filter convolution with S^e. Each filter focusing on difference feature can extract a vector from S^e. In the pooling layer, a max pooling operation is used to create fixed-sized sentence level features.

Convolution. We apply a multi-window and multi-filter convolution operation to S^e. In the single-window architecture, a convolution operation involves a filter $W^c \in \mathbb{R}^{1 \times k(d^w + d^p)}$, which is applied to a window of k words to produce a new feature. For example, a feature c_i is generated by:

$$c_i = f(W^c \cdot emb^{w_i : w_{i+k-1}} + b^c) \tag{2}$$

where $b \in \mathbb{R}^1$ is a bias term, f is the non-linear function ReLU and $emb^{w_i : w_{i+k-1}} \in \mathbb{R}^{k(d^w + d^p) \times 1}$ refer to the concatenation of words $emb^{w_i}, emb^{w_{i+1}}, \cdots, emb^{w_{i+k-1}}$. Then, this filter is applied to each possible window of words in S^e, and we get a feature map

$c = \{c_1, c_2, \cdots, c_n\}$ for S^e. To overcome the issue of referencing words with indices outside of the sentence boundaries, we augment S^e with a special *padding* token replicated $\lfloor \frac{k-1}{2} \rfloor$ times at the beginning and $\lceil \frac{k-1}{2} \rceil$ times at the end. So, the dimension of c is equal to the sentence length. After all filters is applied to S^e, we will get a matrix $C \in \mathbb{R}^{d^c \times n}$, where d^c is the number of filter and n is the length of sentence. In the multi-window architecture, illustrated in Fig. 1. We use multiple sizes of window to focus on multi-granularity level features, and the coarser feature need more filters to extract enough information. In other words, the number d_i^c of the filter which focus on k_i words increases with k_i, and those k_i-size filters can extract a matrix $C_i \in \mathbb{R}^{d_i^c \times n}$ from S^e.

Pooling. After the convolutional layer, the matrix C_i contains local features around each word in the sentence. Then, this pooling layer combines these local features by using a max pooling operation to create a fixed-sized and more abstract higher-level feature vector from matrix C_i. The max aggregating function is popular, as it bears responsibility for identifying the most important or relevant features from the output of the convolutional layer. Concretely, the max pooling operation can be described as:

$$h_j = \max C_i(j, \cdot), \quad 0 \leq j \leq d_i^c \tag{3}$$

where $C_i(j, \cdot)$ denotes the i-th row of matrix C_i. The pooling layer extract a feature vector h_i from matrix C_i, the dimension of h_i is related to the number d_i^c of filter, not the sentence length. All the outputs of the pooling layer are concatenated into the sentence level features $x \in \mathbb{R}^{d^s}$, where d^s equals the number of all multi-window filters.

3.3   Additional Features

We augue some information can't be extracted by the convolution-pooling operation. So, some surface features which are common in coreference resolution are extracted to provide more information for singleton detection. The full set of additional features is as follows:

Type. The type of the mention is divided into 4 categories: "PROPER", "NOMINAL", "PRONOMINAL", and "LIST".

Named entities. Our model also includes named-entity features for all the 18 Onto-Notes entity-types.

Number. The number of the mention has 3 categories: "SINGULAR", "PLURAL", "UNKNOWN".

Length. Like the length features proposed by Clark and Manning [20], the mention length is binned into one of the buckets [1, 2, 3, 4, 5, 6–7, 8–10, 11–14, 15–19, 20+] and then encoded into a one-hot vector.

String match. Whether the mention is exact or relax string match with other mentions.

Those surface features are extracted from text and encoded into one-hot vectors, then those vectors will be concatenated with sentence level features to create the final feature representation $z \in \mathbb{R}^{d^o \times 1}$, where d^o equals the dimension d^s of the sentence level features plus the dimension d^a of the additional features. Then, the scoring function is defined by:

$$s(m) = sigmoid(\mathbf{W}z + b) \tag{4}$$

where $\mathbf{W}$ is a $1 \times d^o$ weight matrix, the $sigmoid(\cdot)$ is a standard nonlinear function and makes $s(m) \in (0, 1)$.

3.4 Training Procedure

Now that we have defined our model, we must decide how to train its parameters $\theta = (\mathbf{W}^e, \mathbf{W}^c, b^c, \mathbf{W}, b)$. In our work, the singleton detection is considered as a logistic regression problem. We choose the logarithmic loss function as the object function. Given t training examples of the form (m_k, a_k^*), the loss function is defined as:

$$L(\theta) = -\frac{1}{t} \sum_{k=1}^{t} \left[a_k^* \log s(m_k) + (1 - a_k^*) \log(1 - s(m_k)) \right] + \lambda \|\theta\|_2 \tag{5}$$

where the relation between m_k and a_k^* is described as:

$$a_k^* = \begin{cases} 1 & \text{if } m_k \text{ is a singleton} \\ 0 & \text{if } m_k \text{ is}'t \text{ a singleton} \end{cases} \tag{6}$$

We update θ using RMSProp and apply dropout with a rate of 0.5 to the concatenation layer. L_2 regularization is used to avoid over-fitting problem.

4 Experiments

4.1 Experimental Setup

Dataset. All experiments use the English portion of the CoNLL 2012 Shared Task dataset [21], which is based on the OntoNotes corpus [22]. The data set contains 3,493 documents with 1.6 million words. The documents are from seven different domains: broadcast conversation (20%), broadcast news (13%), magazine (7%), newswire (21%), telephone conversation (13%), weblogs and newsgroups (15%), and pivot text (11%). We use the standard experimental split of the CoNLL 2012 Shared Task with the training set containing 2,802 documents and 156K annotated mentions, the development set containing 343 documents and 19K annotated mentions, and the test set containing 348 documents and 20K annotated mentions.

In OntoNotes corpus, the singleton mentions are not annotated. So, an extra mention extract step is necessary to get singleton mentions from the data set. We used the rule-based mention detection algorithm from Stanford's rule-based coreference system [10], which first extracted pronouns and maximal NP projections as candidate mentions and then filtered this set with rules. Then, we went through all predicted mentions and select the mentions which were not found in the gold mentions as singleton mentions. In Table 2, we can find that singleton mentions have a large proportion in the total mentions. This proves that the singleton mention is the main difference of predicted mentions and gold mentions.

Table 2. CoNLL-2012 Shared Task data statistics.

Dataset	Docs	Predicted mentions	
		Coreferent	Singleton
Training	2,802	141,509	198,877
Development	343	17,093	25,547
Test	348	18,128	25,553

Settings. There are some hyperparameters in our model, such as the dimension d^w of word embeddings, the dimension d^p of word position embeddings, the dimension d^a of the additional features, the learning rate η, the regularization parameter λ, the window size k and the number d^c of filter. We initialized our word embeddings with 50 dimensional ones produced by word2vec [23] on the Gigaword corpus for English. Like Zeng et al. [15], we choosed $d^p = 5$. All the additional features were encoded in a one-hot vector and concatenated into a 39-dimensional vector. We experimentally studied the effects of the three parameters in our proposed method: learning rate η, regularization parameter λ and the window size k. In Fig. 2, we respectively varied the number of hyper parameters $\{\eta, \lambda, k\}$ and compute the F1 on the CoNLL-2012 development set. At the beginning, the performance became larger and larger with the increase of the regularization parameter λ. While λ is greater than 10^{-9}, the performance starts to fall. When learning rate $\eta = 0.001$, our model got the best performance. the multi-window architecture performs better than the single-window architecture. Table 3 reports all the hyperparameters used in our model.

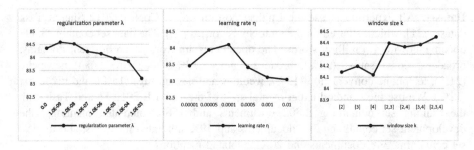

Fig. 2. Effect of hyperparameters.

Table 3. Hyperparameters used in our experiments.

Hyperparameter	d^w	d^p	d^a	η	λ	k	d^c	d^s
Value	50	5	39	0.001	10^{-9}	[2, 3, 4]	[16, 24, 32]	72

4.2   Singleton Detection Results

We compared the results of our system with state-of-the-art singleton detection approaches, the performance measured by F1-score is shown in Table 4. De Marneffe et al. [11] only reported scores on the CoNLL-2012 development set. Haagsma [12] reported scores on the CoNLL-2012 development and test set. To prove the sentence level features extracted from sentence by MMCNN are effective, we built a Surface system which only uses the additional surface features to detect singleton mentions. Our method achieves the best performance among all the compared methods. We also performed a bootstrap resample test $(p < 0.05)$ [24], which indicates that our method significantly outperforms the baseline systems.

Table 4. Comparison with the current state-of-the-art approaches on the CoNLL 2012 dataset. Significant differences (p < 0.05) from the baseline are marked *.

System	Singleton detection		
	Precision	Recall	F1
Marneffe(dev)	81.1	80.8	80.9
Haagsma(dev)	79.77	85.83	82.69
Haagsma(test)	81.57	83.78	82.66
Surface(dev)	80.22	85.30	82.08
Surface(test)	77.54	84.83	81.02
MMCNN(dev)	81.15	87.27	**84.10***
MMCNN(test)	78.35	88.22	**83.00***

4.3   Application to Coreference Resolution

To further evaluate the performance of singleton detection, we incorporated our model into the Berkeley Coreference System, and took the Berkeley Coreference System as a baseline system. Simply, our model was used as a pre-filtering step to coreference resolution. The predicted mentions were fed into our model, then the singleton mentions were filtered out. Like Haagsma [12], this baseline system used the 'FINAL' feature set, and the dataset used in this experiment is the 2012 development set. In our model, the threshold value of 0.95 was chosen so that the singleton classification had a precision of approximately 90%. Table 5 shows the performance of the Berkeley system, and all the coreference results are obtained using the latest version (v8) of the CoNLL scorer [25]. As we can see, this work gets a significant 2.5 percentage point increase over the baseline. This means the singleton detection is meaningful for the coreference resolution. In contrast, Haagsma [12] reported a non-significant performance increase of 0.3 percentage points for the Berkeley. In Table 5, '-' indicates that we could not find published results for those cases.

Table 5. Performance of the Berkeley system on the 2012 development set. Significant differences (p < 0.05) from the baseline are marked *.

System	MUC			B^3			$CEAF_e$			CoNLL
	P	R	F_1	P	R	F_1	P	R	F_1	F_1
Berkeley	73.44	67.67	70.44	63.13	55.54	59.09	56.99	54.21	55.57	61.71
Haagsma	-	-	-	-	-	-	-	-	-	62.02
This work	75.78	70.31	**72.94**	65.42	58.65	**61.85**	59.28	56.46	**57.84**	**64.21***

5   Conclusion

Aiming at reducing the use of hand-designed features and making full use of the information contained in sentence, we explored a novel singleton detection system which uses multi-window and multi-filter convolutional neural network (MMCNN) to extract useful features from sentence, and combined some addintonal features to compute a score for the singleton detection. The results show that singleton detection can improve the performance of coreference resolution, and our system outperforms all the existing singleton detection systems. Comparing to Surface system proves that the sentence level features extracted from sentence by MMCNN are effective.

In future, we will focus on the application of coreference resolution in machine translation. Since the existing works mainly focus on using coreference information to improve pronoun translation, we plan to explore the deeper integration of machine translation and coreference resolution, such as using the coreference information to solve ambiguity problem in machine translation.

Acknowledgment. This research is supported by the National Basic Research Program of China (973 Program, No. 2013CB329303), National Natural Science Foundation of China (NSFC, No. 61502035) and Beijing Advanced Innovation Center for Imaging Technology (BAICIT, No. 2016007).

References

1. Hardmeier, C., Fondazione, M.F., Kessler B.: Modelling pronominal anaphora in statistical machine translation. In: Proceedings of the seventh International Workshop on Spoken Language Translation, pp. 283–289 (2010)
2. Luong, N.Q., Werlen, L.M., Popescu-Belis, A.: Pronoun translation and prediction with or without coreference links. In: The Workshop on Discourse in Machine Translation, pp. 94–100 (2015)
3. Luong, N.Q., Popescu-Belis, A.: Improving pronoun translation by modeling coreference uncertainty. In: Conference on Machine Translation, vol. 1, Research Papers (2016)
4. Werlen, L.M., Popescu-Belis, A.: Using Coreference Links to Improve Spanish-to-English Machine Translation. Idiap (2017)
5. Peng, H., Chang, K.W., Dan, R.: A joint framework for coreference resolution and mention head detection. In: Nineteenth Conference on Computational Natural Language Learning (2015)

6. Chang, K.W., Samdani, R., Rozovskaya, A., Sammons, M., Roth, D.: Illinois-Coref: the UI system in the CoNLL-2012 shared task. In: Joint Conference on EMNLP and CoNLL - Shared Task. Association for Computational Linguistics, pp. 113–117 (2012)
7. Chen, C., Ng, V.: Combining the best of two worlds: a hybrid approach to multilingual coreference resolution. In: Joint Conference on EMNLP and CoNLL - Shared Task. Association for Computational Linguistics, pp. 56–63 (2012)
8. Durrett, G., Klein, D.: Easy victories and uphill battles in coreference resolution. In: Proceedings of the 2013 Conference on Empirical Methods in Natural Language Processing, pp. 1971–1982. ACL (2013)
9. Ma, C., Doppa, J.R., Orr, J.W., Mannem, P., Fern, X.Z., Dietterich, T.G., Tadepalli, P.: Prune-and-score: learning for greedy coreference resolution. In: Conference on Empirical Methods in Natural Language Processing, pp. 2115–2126 (2014)
10. Raghunathan, K., Lee, H., Rangarajan, S., Chambers, N., Surdeanu, M., Jurafsky, D., Manning, C.: A multi-pass sieve for coreference resolution. In: Proceedings of the 2010 Conference on Empirical Methods in Natural Language Processing, pp. 492–501. Association for Computational Linguistics (2010)
11. De Marneffe, M.C., Recasens, M., Potts, C.: Modeling the lifespan of discourse entities with application to coreference resolution. J. Artif. Intell. Res. **52**, 445–475 (2015)
12. Haagsma, H.: Singleton detection using word embeddings and neural networks. In: ACL 2016 (2016)
13. Yuan, B., Chen, Q., Xiang, Y., Wang, X., Ge, L., Liu, Z., Si, X.: A mixed deterministic model for coreference resolution. In: Joint Conference on EMNLP and CoNLL - Shared Task. Association for Computational Linguistics (2012)
14. Björkelund, A., Farkas, R.: Data-driven multilingual coreference resolution using resolver stacking. In: Joint Conference on EMNLP and CoNLL - Shared Task (2012)
15. Zeng, D., Liu, K., Lai, S., Zhou, G., Zhao, J.: Relation classification via convolutional deep neural network. In: COLING (2014)
16. dos Santos, C.N., Xiang, B., Zhou, B.: Classifying relations by ranking with convolutional neural networks. Computer Science (2015)
17. Wang, L., Cao, Z., de Melo, G., Liu, Z.: Relation classification via multi-level attention CNNs. In: Meeting of the Association for Computational Linguistics (2016)
18. Kim, Y.: Convolutional neural networks for sentence classification. Eprint Arxiv (2014)
19. Iida, R., Torisawa, K., Oh, J.H., Kruengkrai, C., Kloetzer, J. Intra-sentential subject zero anaphora resolution using multi-column convolutional neural network. In: Proceedings of EMNLP (2016)
20. Clark, K., Manning, C.D.: Improving coreference resolution by learning entity-level distributed representations. In: Meeting of the Association for Computational Linguistics (2016)
21. Pradhan, S., Moschitti, A., Xue, N., Uryupina, O., Zhang, Y.: CoNLL-2012 shared task: modeling multilingual unrestricted coreference in OntoNotes. In: Joint Conference on EMNLP and CoNLL - Shared Task (2012)
22. Hovy, E., Marcus, M., Palmer, M., Ramshaw, L., Weischedel, R.: OntoNotes: the 90% solution. In: Proceedings of the Human Language Technology Conference of the NAACL, Companion Volume: Short Papers, pp. 57–60. Association for Computational Linguistics (2006)
23. Mikolov, T., Sutskever, I., Chen, K., Corrado, G.S., Dean, J.: Distributed representations of words and phrases and their compositionality. In: Advances in Neural Information Processing Systems, pp. 3111–3119 (2013)
24. Koehn, P.: Statistical significance tests for machine translation evaluation. In: Conference on Empirical Methods in Natural Language Processing, EMNLP, pp. 388–395 (2004)
25. Pradhan, S., Luo, X., Recasens, M., Hovy, E.H., Ng, V., Strube, M.: Scoring coreference partitions of predicted mentions: a reference implementation. In: Meeting of the Association for Computational Linguistics (2014)

A Method of Unknown Words Processing for Neural Machine Translation Using HowNet

Shaotong Li, JinAn Xu$^{(\boxtimes)}$, Yujie Zhang, and Yufeng Chen

School of Computer and Information Technology,
Beijing Jiaotong University, Beijing, China
{shaotongli,jaxu,yjzhang,chenyf}@bjtu.edu.cn

Abstract. An inherent weakness of neural machine translation (NMT) systems is their inability to correctly translate unknown words. Traditional unknown words processing methods are usually based on word vectors trained on large scale of monolingual corpus. Replacing the unknown words according to the similarity of word vectors. However, it suffers from two weaknesses: Firstly, the resulting vectors of unknown words are not of high quality; Secondly, it is difficult to deal with polysemous words. This paper proposes an unknown word processing method by integrating HowNet. Using the concepts and sememes in HowNet to seek the replacement words of unknown words. Experimental results show that our proposed method can not only improves the performance of NMT, but also provides some advantages compared with the traditional unknown words processing methods.

Keywords: NMT · Unknown words · HowNet · Concept · Sememe

End-to-End NMT is a kind of machine translation method proposed in recent years [1–4]. Most of the NMT systems are based on the encoder-decoder framework, the encoder encodes the source sentence into a vector, and the decoder decodes the vector into the target sentence. Compared with the traditional statistical machine translation (SMT), NMT has many advantages, and has shown greatly performance in many translation tasks.

But NMT still has the problem of unknown words which is caused by the limited vocabulary scale. In order to control the temporal and spatial expenses of the model, NMT usually uses small vocabularies in the source side and the target side [5]. The words that are not in the vocabulary are unknown words, which will be replaced by an "*UNK*" symbol. A feasible method to solve this problem is to find out the substitute in-vocabulary words of the unknown words. Li et al. proposed a replacing method based on word vector similarity [5], the unknown words are replaced by the synonyms in the vocabulary through the cosine distance of the word vector and the language model. However, there are some unavoidable problems with this method. Firstly, the vectors of rare words are difficult to train; Secondly, the trained word vectors cannot express various semantics of the polysemous words and cannot adapt to the replacement of the polysemous words in different contexts.

To solve these problems, this paper proposes an unknown words processing method based on HowNet. This method uses HowNet's concepts and sememes as well

© Springer Nature Singapore Pte Ltd. 2017
D.F. Wong and D. Xiong (Eds.): CWMT 2017, CCIS 787, pp. 20–29, 2017.
https://doi.org/10.1007/978-981-10-7134-8_3

as language models to calculate the semantic similarity between words and select the best alternative words to replace the unknown words.

Experiments on English to Chinese translation tasks demonstrate that our proposed method can achieve more than 2.89 BLEU points over the baseline system, and also outperform the traditional method based on word vector similarity by nearly 0.7 BLEU points.

The main contributions of this paper are shown as follows:

- An external bilingual semantic dictionary is integrated to solve the problem of unknown words in NMT.
- The semantic concepts and sememes in HowNet are used to obtain the replacement word, which can solve the problem of rare words and polysemous words better.
- A similarity model which integrates the language models and HowNet is proposed. It not only ensures that the replacement words are close to the unknown words in semantic level, but also keeps the semantic completeness of the source sentence as much as possible.

1 NMT and the Problem of Unknown Words

In this section, we will introduce NMT and the impact of the unknown words on NMT.

1.1 Neural Machine Translation with Attention

Most of the proposed NMT systems are based on the encoder-decoder framework and attention mechanism which learn to soft-align and translate jointly [4].

The encoder consists of a bidirectional recurrent neural network (Bi-RNN), which can read a source sequence $X(x_1, ..., x_t)$ and generate a sequence of forward hidden states $(\vec{h}_t, ..., \vec{h}_\tau)$ and a sequence of backward hidden states $(\overleftarrow{h}_t, ..., \overleftarrow{h}_t)$. We obtain the annotation h_i for each source word x_i by concatenating the forward hidden state $\vec{h}_i$ and the backward hidden state $\overleftarrow{h}_i$.

The decoder consists of a recurrent neural network (RNN), an attention network and a logical regression network. At each time step i, the RNN generates the hidden state s_i based on the previous hidden state s_{i-1}, the previous predicted word y_{i-1}, and the context vector c_i which is calculated as a weighted sum of the source annotations by the attention network. Then the logical regression network predicts the target word y_i.

1.2 The Problem of Unknown Words

When predicting the target word at each time step, it is necessary to generate the probability of all the words in the target vocabulary. Therefore, the output dimension of the logical regression network is equal to the target vocabulary size, the total computational complexity will grow almost proportional to the vocabulary size. So train the model with the whole vocabulary is infeasible, which leads to the problem of unknown words caused by the limitation of the vocabulary size.

In NMT system, the unknown words mainly lead to two problems: Firstly, the NMT model is difficult to learn the representation and the appropriate translation of the unknown words, the parameter quality of the neural network is poor. Secondly, the existence of the unknown words increases the ambiguity of the source sentence, affects the accuracy of attention network and the quality of translation result.

2 Our Method

This paper proposes an unknown words processing method with HowNet. The framework of our method is shown in Fig. 1.

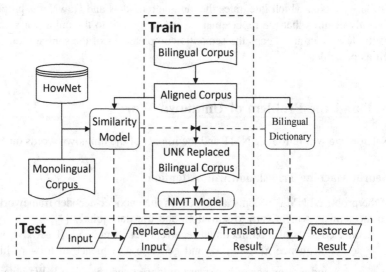

Fig. 1. Framework of our unknown words processing method

In the training phase, we will first learn a similarity model from the monolingual corpus and HowNet, which is used to evaluate the semantic similarity between words. At the same time, we need to align the bilingual corpus and extract a bilingual dictionary. Then we use the similarity model and bilingual dictionary to replace unknown words both in source side and target side. Finally, we train a NMT model with the replaced bilingual corpus.

In the testing phrase, we will first replace the unknown words with the similarity model. After replacement, we use the trained NMT model to translate the replaced input sentences. During translating, the alignment probabilities of each target word are obtained by the attention network. Finally, the translation of replaced words will be restored by the alignment probabilities and the bilingual dictionary.

This section mainly introduces HowNet and the details of our proposed method.

2.1 HowNet

HowNet[1] is a widely used computable Chinese and English semantic dictionary. In HowNet, the formal description of words is organized in three layers: "word", "concept", and "sememe". The words are expressed by concepts, concepts are defined by sememes which are well-designed by the author of HowNet. That is to say, all the concepts are made up of different combinations of sememes.

"Concept" is a description of lexical semantics. Each word can be expressed as several concepts. "Concept" is described by a kind of knowledge expressing language, which is composed by sememes. "Sememe" is the basic semantic unit, all the sememes are organized into a hierarchical tree structure by the Hypernym-Hyponym relations.

We use HowNet 2008 in our experiments, there are 1700 sememes, 28925 concepts, 96744 Chinese words and 93467 English words.

2.2 Similarity Model

The replacement words should not only be close to the unknown words in semantics, but also should keep the semantics of the original sentence as much as possible. Therefore, this paper defines a semantic similarity model by integrating the language models and HowNet, to calculate the semantic similarity between the in-vocabulary words and the unknown words, and then selects the best replacement words.

We trained a 3-gram language models in our experiment, so for an unknown word w_i and its candidate replacement word w_i', where i refers the position of w in the sentence, the score on the 3-gram language model is defined as formula 1:

$$Score_{3\text{-}gram}(w_i', w_i) = \frac{p(w_i' \mid w_{i-1}, w_{i-2}) + p(w_{i+1} \mid w_i', w_{i-1}) + p(w_{i+2} \mid w_{i+1}, w_i')}{3} \quad (1)$$

We use the method proposed by Liu and Li [6] to calculate the semantic similarity of word pair (w_i', w_i) in HowNet, which is defined as:

$$Sim_{HowNet}(w_1, w_2) = \max_{i=1...n, j=1...m} \sum_{I=1}^{4} \beta_I \prod_J^I Sim_J(S_{1i}, S_{2j}) \quad (2)$$

where S_{1i} and S_{2j} are all the corresponding concepts of w_1 and w_2, $Sim(S_{1i}, S_{2j})$ are the partial similarities. β are adjustable parameters. Details of this formula are described in reference [6].

This similarity calculation method defines the similarity between words as the maximum similarity of all corresponding concepts. Converting the similarity calculation between words to the similarity calculation between concepts. Then concept similarity is decomposed into the combination of some sememe similarities through the semantic expression of concept. The sememe similarity is calculated by semantic distance between sememes which is obtained by the Hypernym-Hyponym relations.

---

[1] http://www.keenage.com/.

This method has the following advantages: Firstly, the concepts can express various semantics of polysemous words; secondly, as long as the unknown words are included in HowNet, the difference between rare words and common words can be eliminated effectively.

The semantic similarity of the word pair (w_i', w_i) is finally defined as formula 3:

$$Sim(w_i', w_i) = \sqrt{Score_{3\text{-}gram}(w_i', w_i) \cdot Sim_{HowNet}(w_i', w_i)} \tag{3}$$

In word alignment phrase, we only reserve the aligned pair with the highest probability for each word. So the aligned bilingual corpus only contains aligned word pairs with one-to-one mapping or one-to-null mapping. Therefore, when replacing aligned word pairs which contains unknown words, we need to handle three cases:

- *Both source side and target side are unknown words*: In this case, we must consider bilingual word similarity. That is to say, only the translation pair which is similar to the original pair in both source and target side will be selected. For an aligned word pair (s_i, t_j), the score to replace them with alternative pair (s_i', t_j') is calculated as formula 4:

$$Score = \frac{Sim(s_i, s_i') + Sim(t_j, t_j')}{2} \tag{4}$$

- *One side is unknown word and another side is in-vocabulary word*: In this case, we only replace the unknown word s_i. But we should also consider bilingual word similarity. Only the word which is similar to the original word and its translation is similar to the align word will be selected. So we will firstly get the translation of alternative replacement word s_i' which is defined as $T_{s_i'}$ by the bilingual dictionary. And calculate the replacement score with formula 5:

$$Score = \frac{Sim(s_i, s_i') + Sim(t_j, T_{s_i'})}{2} \tag{5}$$

- *One side is unknown word and another side is null*: In this case, we only consider monolingual word similarity, so we will simply regard the similarity of unknown word w_i and it's alternative replacement word w_i' as the replacement score:

$$Score = Sim(w_i, w_i') \tag{6}$$

Finally, the word pair or word in the in-vocabulary words with highest replacement score will be chosen to replace the unknown words.

2.3   Restore Unknown Words

NMT model is a sequence to sequence model, we can only find the most likely alignment through the attention network. However, the performance of the attention network in NMT model is very unstable. In order to reduce the effect of alignment errors, a judging operation is added to the alignment: We align the words in the training corpus with GIZA++ [7] to get a bilingual dictionary, which will contain all words in training corpus and their translations. For the word t_i in the output sentence, if t_i aligns to a replaced word s_j, the previously obtained bilingual dictionary will be used to determine the correctness of the alignment: If word pair (s_i, t_i) is in the bilingual dictionary, then the alignment is correct, then replace t_i with the translation of original source word. Otherwise t_i will be kept in the output sentence.

3 Experiments

Since HowNet is a Chinese and English semantic dictionary, we verify our method on the English to Chinese translation task.

3.1 Settings

The bilingual data used to train NMT model is selected from the CWMT2015[2] English-Chinese news corpus, including 1.6 million sentence pairs. The development set and test set are officially provided by CWMT2015, each with 1000 sentences. In order to shorten the training time, the sentence pairs longer than 50 words either on the source side or on the target side will be filtered out. The word alignment is also carried out on the training set. The language models and the word vectors will be trained on the monolingual data, which contains 5 million sentences selected from the CWMT2015 English-Chinese news corpus, both on source language and target language.

We use the BLEU score [8] to evaluate the translation results.

3.2 Training Details

The hyper parameters of our NMT system are described as follows: the vocabulary size of the source side is limited to 20k, and the target side, 30k. The number of hidden units is 512 for both encoder and decoder. The word embedding dimension of the source and target words is 512. The parameters are updated with Adadelt algorithm [9]. The Dropout method [10] is used at the readout layer, and the dropout rate is set as 0.5.

3.3 Comparative Experiments and Main Results

There are 5 different systems in our comparative experiments:

1. Moses [11]: An open-source phrase-based SMT system with default configuration.
2. RNNSearch: Our baseline NMT system with improved attention mechanism [12].
3. PosUnk: Add a method proposed by Luong et al. [13] to the baseline NMT system in order to process unknown words.
4. w2v&lm_restore: Based on our baseline NMT system, use the method proposed by Li et al. [5] to replace the unknown words based on word vectors and the language

[2] http://www.ai-ia.ac.cn/cwmt2015/.

models. The word vectors are trained by word2vec [14] toolkit, and the 3-gram language models with modified Kneser-Ney smoothing is trained by SRILM [15].
5. hn&lm_restore: Based on the baseline NMT system, our method will use HowNet and the language models to replace the unknown words. The language models used are the same as the language models used in system 4.

The main experimental results are shown in Table 1.

Table 1. BLEU scores (%) of different systems

System	Dev set	Test set	Average
Moses	27.42	24.48	25.95
RNNSearch	25.71	23.22	24.47
PosUnk	27.58	24.89	26.24
w2v&lm_restore	27.56	25.02	26.29
hn&lm_restore	26.03	23.68	24.86

As we can see, our system (hn&lm_restore) performs poor on the experiment data. It slightly improves the baseline NMT, while the performance is worse than the other unknown words processing methods. The reason is that more than two-thirds of the unknown words in the experiment data are not contained in HowNet, these unknown words cannot be replaced by our method. To make our method more effective, we select another experiment data from the CWMT2015 English-Chinese news corpus, in which most of the unknown words are contained in HowNet. We refer this data as HowNet adapted data. The new data include the training set of 1 million sentences, the development set of 1000 sentences and test set of 1000 sentences. The experimental results on HowNet adapted data are shown in Table 2.

Table 2. BLEU scores (%) of different systems on HowNet adapted data

System	Dev set	Test set	Average
Moses	24.21	26.55	25.38
RNNSearch	23.76	26.81	25.29
PosUnk	25.62	28.24	26.93
w2v&lm_restore	26.16	28.80	27.48
hn&lm_restore	**26.97**	**29.39**	**28.18**

On HowNet adapted data, our system (hn&lm_restore) outperforms the baseline system (RNNSearch) by 2.89 BLEU on average; In addition, it surpasses the NMT system which add a simple unknown word processing module (PosUnk) by 1.25 BLEU points, it significantly improves the NMT system of traditional method (w2v&lm_restore) by 0.7 BLEU points.

Clearly, our method is effective on HowNet adapted corpus, these results show the effectiveness of our proposed method. As HowNet continues to expand and improve, our approach will become more useful on more corpus.

3.4   Comparison of Translating Details

Here we compare the translating details of our system with other systems, we mainly analyze the translating process of unknown words. The translation instances are shown in Table 3.

The main advantage of our system is that the replacement words selected by our system are more appropriate. In eg1 and eg2, the unknown words are word with tense (*amazingly*) or compound word (*never-ending*). These unknown words break the semantic continuity of source sentences. What's worse, these words are rare words,

Table 3. Translation instances table

Eg1	Source	The manufacturer thinks this kind of shoes is **amazingly(unk)** cool .
	Reference	厂商 认为 这 种 鞋 非常 的 酷 。
	RNNSearch	制造商 认为 这 种 鞋 是 <UNK> 的 。
	PosUnk	制造商 认为 这 种 鞋 是 非常 的 。
	Replaced source(w2v&lm)	The manufacturer thinks this kind of shoes is **though** cool.
	w2v&lm	制造商 认为 这 种 鞋 尽管 很 酷 。
	w2v&lm+restore	制造商 认为 这 种 鞋 非常 很 酷 。
	Replaced source(hn&lm)	The manufacturer thinks this kind of shoes is **very** cool.
	hn&lm	制造商 认为 这 种 鞋 很 酷 。
	hn&lm+restore	制造商 认为 这 种 鞋 非常 酷 。
Eg2	Source	Outside the window, all that's left to see is **never-ending(unk)** green.
	Reference	窗外 ， 能 看见 的 只 剩下 连绵 的 绿 。
	RNNSearch	在 窗户 外面 的 时候 看到 的 是 <UNK> 的 绿色
	PosUnk	在 窗户 外面 的 时候 看到 的 是 连绵 的 绿色
	Replaced source(w2v&lm)	Outside the window, all that's left to see is **cognition** green.
	w2v&lm	在 窗户 外面 的 时候 看到 的 是 认知 绿色 的 。
	w2v&lm+restore	在 窗户 外面 的 时候 看到 的 是 连绵 绿色 的 。
	Replaced source(hn&lm)	Outside the window, all that's left to see is **constant** green.
	hn&lm	窗 外 所有 的 可以 看到 的 东西 是 不断 的 绿色 。
	hn&lm+restore	窗 外 所有 的 可以 看到 的 东西 是 连绵 的 绿色 。
Eg3	Source	The us army in Europe have currently fallen to **110,000(unk)** people .
	Reference	目前 驻 欧 美军 已 降至 11万 人 。
	RNNSearch	在 欧洲 的 美国 军队 目前 已 落 到 <UNK> 人 。
	PosUnk	在 欧洲 的 美国 军队 目前 已 落 到 11万 人 。
	Replaced source(w2v&lm)	The us army in Europe have currently fallen to **1,000** people .
	w2v&lm	在 欧洲 的 美国 军队 目前 已 下降 到 1000 人 。
	w2v&lm+restore	在 欧洲 的 美国 军队 目前 已 下降 到 11万 人 。
	Replaced source(hn&lm)	The us army in Europe have currently fallen to **110,000(unk)** people .
	hn&lm	在 欧洲 的 美国 军队 目前 已 落 到 <UNK> 人 。
	hn&lm+restore	在 欧洲 的 美国 军队 目前 已 落 到 <UNK> 人 。

which means their word vectors are not well trained. So that traditional replacement methods change the original meaning of source sentences, affect the subsequent translations, result in over translation or unfluent translation.

However, these rare words are contained in HowNet. Our proposed method finds more appropriate replacement words, keeps the original meaning of source sentences better and provides less impact on subsequent translations. After restoring, we can finally obtain translations which are very close to the references.

Although our method can handle most of the unknown words, there still remain some unsolved unknown words. In eg3, the number *110,000* is not contained in HowNet, our method cannot deal with this kind of items. For this case, we can only replace unknown words in post processing.

4   Conclusion and Future Work

This paper proposes an unknown words processing method in NMT by integrating concepts and sememes in HowNet and language models. This method has advantages in dealing with rare words and polysemous words, it not only improves the translation of the unknown words in NMT, but also ensures the semantic completeness of the original sentence. Experiments on English to Chinese translation show that our method not only achieves a significant improvement over the baseline NMT, but also provides some advantages compared with the traditional unknown words processing methods.

Our future work mainly contains two aspects. Firstly, our proposed method relies on the coverage of HowNet on corpus, improving this coverage will be leaved as our future work. Secondly, the replacement method proposed in this paper is limited to the replacement of word level, we are going to challenge the phrase level method.

Acknowledgments. The authors are supported by the National Nature Science Foundation of China (Contract 61370130 and 61473294), and Beijing Natural Science Foundation under Grant No. 4172047, and the Fundamental Research Funds for the Central Universities (2015JBM033), and the International Science and Technology Cooperation Program of China under grant No. 2014DFA11350.

References

1. Kalchbrenner, N., Blunsom, P.: Recurrent continuous translation models (2013)
2. Sutskever, I., Vinyals, O., Le, Q.V.: Sequence to sequence learning with neural networks. Adv. Neural. Inf. Process. Syst. **4**, 3104–3112 (2014)
3. Luong, M.T., Pham, H., Manning, C.D.: On the properties of neural machine translation: encoder-decoder approaches. Computer Science (2014)
4. Bahdanau, D., Cho, K., Bengio, Y.: Neural machine translation by jointly learning to align and translate. Computer Science (2014)
5. Li, X., Zhang, J., Zong, C.: Towards zero unknown word in neural machine translation. In: International Joint Conference on Artificial Intelligence, pp. 2852–2858. AAAI Press (2016)
6. Liu, Q., Li, S.: Word similarity computing based on Hownet. Comput. Linguist. Chin. Lang. Process. **7**(2), 59–76 (2002)

7. Och, F.J., Ney, H.: A Systematic Comparison of Various Statistical Alignment Models. MIT Press, Cambridge (2003)
8. Papineni, K., Roukos, S., Ward, T., Zhu, W.-J.: BLEU: a method for auto matice valuation of machine translation. In: Proceedings of 40th Annual Meeting of the Association for Computational Linguistics, Philadelphia, Pennsylvania, USA, July 2002, pp. 311–318 (2002)
9. Zeiler, M.D.: ADADELTA: an adaptive learning rate method. Computer Science (2012)
10. Srivastava, N., Hinton, G., Krizhevsky, A., et al.: Dropout: a simple way to prevent neural networks from overfitting. J. Mach. Learn. Res. 15(1), 1929–1958 (2014)
11. Collins, M., Koehn, P.: Clause restructuring for statistical machine translation. In: Meeting on Association for Computational Linguistics. Association for Computational Linguistics, pp. 531–540 (2005)
12. Meng, F., Lu, Z., Li, H., et al.: Interactive attention for neural machine translation (2016)
13. Luong, M.T., Sutskever, I., Le, Q.V., et al.: Addressing the rare word problem in neural machine translation. Bull. Univ. Agric. Sci. Vet. Med. Cluj-Napoca 27(2), 82–86 (2014)
14. Mikolov, T., Sutskever, I., Chen, K., et al.: Distributed representations of words and phrases and their compositionality. Adv. Neural. Inf. Process. Syst. 26, 3111–3119 (2013)
15. Stolcke, A.: SRILM—an extensible language modeling toolkit. In: International Conference on Spoken Language Processing, pp. 901–904 (2002)

Word, Subword or Character? An Empirical Study of Granularity in Chinese-English NMT

Yining Wang[1], Long Zhou[1], Jiajun Zhang[1(✉)], and Chengqing Zong[1,2]

[1] National Laboratory of Pattern Recognition, CASIA,
University of Chinese Academy of Sciences, Beijing, China
{yining.wang,long.zhou,jjzhang,cqzong}@nlpr.ia.ac.cn
[2] CAS Center for Excellence in Brain Science and Intelligence Technology,
Beijing, China

Abstract. Neural machine translation (NMT) becomes a new approach to machine translation and is proved to outperform conventional statistical machine translation (SMT) across a variety of language pairs. Most existing NMT systems operate with a fixed vocabulary, but translation is an open-vocabulary problem. Hence, previous works mainly handle rare and unknown words by using different translation granularities, such as character, subword, and hybrid word-character. While translation involving Chinese has been proved to be one of the most difficult tasks, there is no study to demonstrate which translation granularity is the most suitable for Chinese in NMT. In this paper, we conduct an extensive comparison using Chinese-English NMT as a case study. Furthermore, we discuss the advantages and disadvantages of various translation granularities in detail. Our experiments show that subword model performs best for Chinese-to-English translation while hybrid word-character model is most suitable for English-to-Chinese translation.

Keywords: Neural machine translation · Translation granularity · Subword model · Character model

1 Introduction

Neural machine translation (NMT) proposed by Kalchbrenner and Blunsom [9] and Sutskever et al. [20] has achieved significant progress in recent years. Unlike traditional statistical machine translation (SMT) [3,11,23] which contains multiple separately tuned components, NMT builds an end-to-end framework to model the entire translation process. For several language pairs, NMT has already achieved better translation performance than SMT [8,22].

Conventional NMT system limits the vocabulary to a modest-sized vocabulary in both sides and a large amount of out-of-vocabulary words will be represented by a special **UNK** symbol. However, the process of training and decoding is often conducted on a open vocabulary, in which an obvious problem is that NMT model is incapable of translating rare words. In particular, if a source word

© Springer Nature Singapore Pte Ltd. 2017
D.F. Wong and D. Xiong (Eds.): CWMT 2017, CCIS 787, pp. 30–42, 2017.
https://doi.org/10.1007/978-981-10-7134-8_4

is outside the source vocabulary or its translation is outside the target vocabulary, the model will not be able to generate proper translation for this word during decoding. Both Sutskever et al. [20] and Bahdanau et al. [1] have observed that sentences with many out-of-vocabulary words tend to be translated much more poorly than sentences mainly containing frequent words.

To address this problem, many researchers propose a broad category of approaches, in which they employ different translation granularities. Most of these are below the word level, e.g. characters [4], hybrid word-characters [13,22], and more intelligent subwords [19,22]. Besides, pioneering studies [8,22] demonstrate that translation tasks involving Chinese is one of the most difficult problems in NMT systems. However, there is no study that shows which translation granularities is suitable for Chinese-to-English and English-to-Chinese translation tasks.

In this work, we make an empirical comparison of different translation granularities for bidirectional English-Chinese translation tasks. In addition, we analyze the impact of these strategies on the translation results in detail. We demonstrate that subword model is the best translation granularity for Chinese-to-English NMT while hybrid word-character model is most suitable for English-to-Chinese translation, and our experiment shows that all subword methods are not bound by the vocabulary size. To the best of our knowledge, this is the first work on an empirical comparison of various translation granularities for bidirectional Chinese-English translations.

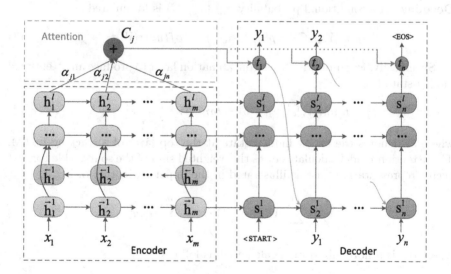

Fig. 1. The architecture of neural machine translation model.

2 Neural Machine Translation

Our models are based on an encoder-decoder architecture with attention mechanism proposed by Luong et al. [14], which utilizes stacked LSTM layers for both encoder and decoder as illustrated in Fig. 1. In this section, we make a review of NMT framework.

First, the NMT encodes the source sentence $X = (x_1, x_2, \ldots, x_m)$ into a sequence of context vector representation $C = (h_1, h_2, \ldots, h_m)$. Then, the NMT decodes from the context vector representation C and generates target translation $Y = (y_1, y_2, \ldots, y_n)$ one word each time by maximizing the probability of $p(y_j|y_{<j}, C)$. Next, We review the encoder and decoder frameworks briefly.

Encoder: The context vector representation $C = (h_1^l, h_2^l, \ldots, h_m^l)$ are generated by the encoder using l stacked LSTM layers. Bi-directional connections are used for the bottom encoder layer, and h_i^1 is a concatenation vector as shown in Eq. (1):

$$h_i^1 = \begin{bmatrix} \overrightarrow{h}_i^1 \\ \overleftarrow{h}_i^1 \end{bmatrix} = \begin{bmatrix} LSTM(\overrightarrow{h}_{i-1}^1, x_i) \\ LSTM(\overleftarrow{h}_{i-1}^1, x_i) \end{bmatrix} \tag{1}$$

All other encoder layers are unidirectional, and h_i^k is calculated as follows:

$$h_i^k = LSTM(h_{i-1}^k, h_i^{k-1}) \tag{2}$$

Decoder: The conditional probability $p(y_j|y_{<j}, C)$ is formulated as

$$p(y_j|Y_{<j}, C) = p(y_j|Y_{<j}, c_j) = softmax(W_s t_j) \tag{3}$$

Specifically, we employ a simple concatenation layer to produce an attentional hidden state t_j:

$$t_j = tanh(W_c[s_j^l; c_j] + b) = tanh(W_c^1 s_j^l + W_c^2 c_j + b) \tag{4}$$

where s_j^l denotes the target hidden state at the top layer of a stacking LSTM. The attention model calculates c_j as the weighted sum of the source-side context vector representation, just as illustrated in the upper left corner of Fig. 1.

$$c_j = \sum_{i=1}^{m} ATT(s_j^l, h_i^l) \cdot h_i^l = \sum_{i=1}^{m} \alpha_{ji} h_i^l \tag{5}$$

where α_{ji} is a normalized item calculated as follows:

$$\alpha_{ji} = \frac{exp(h_i^l \cdot s_j^l)}{\sum_{i'} exp(h_{i'}^l \cdot s_j^l)} \tag{6}$$

s_j^k is computed by using the following formula:

$$s_j^k = LSTM(s_{j-1}^k, s_j^{k-1}) \tag{7}$$

If $k = 1$, s_j^1 will be calculated by combining t_{j-1} as feed input [14]:

$$s_j^1 = LSTM(s_{j-1}^1, y_{j-1}, t_{j-1}) \tag{8}$$

Given the bilingual training data $D = \{(X^{(z)}, Y^{(z)})\}_{z=1}^Z$, all parameters of the attention-based NMT are optimized to maximize the following conditional log-likelihood:

$$L(\theta) = \frac{1}{Z} \sum_{z=1}^{Z} \sum_{j=1}^{n} log p(y_j^{(z)} | y_{<j}^{(z)}, X^{(z)}, \theta) \tag{9}$$

3   Description of Different Translation Granularities

We revisit how the source and target sentences (X and Y) are represented in NMT. For the source side of any given training corpus, we scan through the whole corpus to build a vocabulary V_x of unique tokens. A source sentence $X = (x_1, x_2, \ldots, x_m)$ is then built as a sequence of the integer indices. The target sentence is similarly transformed into a target sequence of integer indices.

The property of NMT allows us great freedom in the choice of token units, and we can segment sentences in different ways. In this section, we will elaborate on four proposed approaches about the choice of translation granularities.

Sentence:	龙年新春，繁花似锦的深圳处处洋溢着欢乐祥和的气氛 。
Word:	龙年 新春 ， 繁花似锦 的 深圳 处处 洋溢 着 欢乐 祥和 的 气氛 。
Character:	龙 年 新 春 ， 繁 花 似 锦 的 深 圳 处 处 洋 溢 着 欢 乐 祥 和 的 气 氛 。
Hybrid :	\<B>龙 \<E>年 新春 ， \<B>繁 \<M>花 \<M>似 \<E>锦 的 深圳 处处 洋溢 着 欢乐 祥和 的 气氛 。
BPE:	龙年 新春 ， 繁花@@ 似@@ 锦 的 深圳 处处 洋溢 着 欢乐 祥和 的 气氛 。
Wordpiece:	龙 年 _新春 ， ， 繁花 似 锦 _的 _深圳 _处处 _洋 溢 着 _欢乐 _祥 和 _的 _气氛 _。

Fig. 2. An example of different translation granularities

3.1   Character Level

This translation granularity is easy to implement. For this granularity, what we have to do is split the sentence into a sequence of characters. However, the character-level modeling on the English side is more challenging, as the network has to be able to deal with long and coherent sequence of characters. In this case, the number of characters is often 300–1000 symbols long, where the size of the state space grows exponentially. Therefore, this is a great challenge for us to handle.

Besides, the alphabet of English is only consist of 26 letters, in which the vocabulary of English side is too small. Considering these facts, we only separate the Chinese side sentences into characters rather than both sides. Figure 2 shows an example of this translation granularity for character level.

3.2 Hybrid Word-Characters Level

In regular word-based NMT, for all words outside the source vocabulary, one feeds the universal embedding representing **UNK** as input to the encoder. This is problematic because it discards valuable information about the source word. To address that, hybrid word-character approach will be adopted. In this part, we will introduce this granularity in detail.

Unlike in the conventional word model where out-of-vocabulary words are collapsed into a single **UNK** symbol, we convert these words into the sequence of constituent characters. Special prefixes are prepended to the characters. The purpose of the prefixes is to show the location of the characters in a word, and to distinguish them from normal in-vocabulary characters. There are three prefixes: $\langle \mathbf{B} \rangle$, $\langle \mathbf{M} \rangle$, and $\langle \mathbf{E} \rangle$, indicating beginning of the word, middle of the word and end of the word, respectively. During decoding, the output may also contain sequences of special tokens. With the prefixes, it is trivial to reverse the tokenization to the original words as part of a post-processing step. Using this approach, in Fig. 2, we can see the word "龙年" is segmented into "⟨B⟩龙 ⟨E⟩年", and the word "繁花似锦" is segmented into "⟨B⟩繁 ⟨M⟩花 ⟨M⟩似 ⟨E⟩锦".

3.3 Subword Level

Considering languages with productive word formation processes such as agglutination and compounding, translation models require mechanisms that segment the sentence below the word level (In this paper, we call this level of symbols as subword units). In this part, we will introduce the two different methods of translation granularity on subword level.

BPE Method. Byte pair encoding (BPE) [5] is a compression algorithm. This simple data compression technique iteratively replaces the most frequent pair of bytes in a sequence with a single, unused byte. This compression method is first introduced into translation granularity by Sennrich et al. [19]. In this approach, instead of merging frequent pairs of bytes, characters or character sequences will be merged.

A detailed introduction of algorithm in learning BPE operations is showed in Sennrich et al. [19]. During decoding time, each word first split into sequences of characters, then learned operation will be applied to merge the characters into larger, known symbols. For BPE method, a special symbol is also needed to indicate the merging position. In Fig. 2, the word "繁花似锦" is segmented into three subword units, and the first three units are appended a special suffix "@@". In decoding step, the translation results contain the special tokens as well. With these suffixes, we can recover the output easily.

WPM Method. The wordpiece model (WPM) implementation is initially developed to solve a Japanese/Korean segmentation problem for the speech recognition system [18]. This approach is completely data-driven and guaranteed to generate a deterministic segmentation for any possible sequence of characters, which is similar to the above method.

The wordpiece model is generated using a data-driven approach to maximize the language-model likelihood of the training data, given an evolving word definition. The training method of WPM is described in more detail in Schuster and Nakajima [18]. As shown in Fig. 2, a special symbol is only prepended at the beginning of the words. In this case, the words "龙年", "繁花似锦", "洋溢" and "祥和" are split into subwords, and the rest words remain the same except for a special prefix "_".

4 Experiments

4.1 Dataset

We perform all these translation granularities on the NIST bidirectional Chinese-English translation tasks. The evaluation metric is BLEU [17] as calculated by the `multi-bleu.perl` script.

Our training data consists of 2.09M sentence pairs extracted from LDC corpus[1]. Table 1 shows the detailed statistics of our training data. To test different approaches on Chinese-to-English translation task, we use NIST 2003(MT03) dataset as the validation set, and NIST 2004(MT04), NIST 2005(MT05), NIST 2006(MT06) datasets as our test sets. For English-to-Chinese translation task, we also use NIST 2003(MT03) dataset as the validation set, and NIST 2008(MT08) will be used as test set.

Table 1. The characteristics of our training dataset on the LDC corpus.

Corpora		Chinese	English
LDC corpora	#Sent.	2.09M	
	#Word	43.14M	47.73M
	Vocab	0.39M	0.23M

---

[1] The corpora include LDC2000T50, LDC2002T01, LDC2002E18, LDC2003E07, LDC2003E14, LDC2003T17 and LDC2004T07.

4.2   Training Details

We build the described models modified from the Zoph_RNN[2] toolkit which is written in C++/CUDA and provides efficient training across multiple GPUs. Our training procedure and hyper parameter choices are similar to those used by Luong et al. [14]. In the NMT architecture as illustrated in Fig. 1, the encoder has three stacked LSTM layers including a bidirectional layer, followed by a global attention layer, and the decoder contains two stacked LSTM layers followed by the softmax layer.

The word embedding dimension and the size of hidden layers are all set to 1000. We limit the maximum length in training corpus to 120. Parameter optimization is performed using both stochastic gradient descent (SGD) method and Adam method [10]. For the first three epoches, We train using the Adam optimizer and a fixed learning rate of 0.001 without decay. For the remaining six epoches, we train using SGD, and we set learning rate to 0.1 at the beginning and halve the threshold while the perplexity go up on the development set. We set minibatch size to 128. Dropout was also applied on each layer to avoid overfitting, and the dropout rate is set to 0.2. At test time, we employ beam search with beam size b = 12.

4.3   Data Segmentation

For Chinese word segmentation, we use our in-house segmentation tools. For English corpus, the training data is tokenized with the Moses tokenizer. We carry out Chinese-to-English translation experiment on 30k vocabulary and 15k vocabulary for both sides respectively, and we also conduct English-to-Chinese translation experiment on 30k vocabulary size. The word level translation granularity is set to our baseline method.

For character level, we only segment the Chinese sentences into characters and the English sentences remain the same. For hybrid word-characters level, we segment training corpus for both sides. We rank the word frequency from greatest to least in training corpus, and in order to prevent the pollution from the very rare word, we have to set a segmentation point relatively higher. For 30k vocabulary, the word frequency below 64 is segmented into characters on Chinese side, and the segmentation point is set to 22 on English side. For 15k vocabulary, we set the segmentation point to 350 and 96 on Chinese side and English side respectively.

For subword level, two different approaches are used. In BPE method[3], the number of merge operations is set to 30000 on 30k vocabulary size and 15000 on 15k vocabulary size. For Chinese sentences, we segment the training corpus using our in-house segmentation tools first, and then we can apply the BPE method same as English sentences. Considering the essence of WPM method[4], we do not have to segment words for Chinese and tokenize sentences for English.

---

[2] https://github.com/isi-nlp/Zoph_RNN.
[3] https://github.com/rsennrich/subword-nmt.
[4] https://github.com/google/sentencepiece.

That is to say, we can train the WPM without pre-processing step. Hence, for WPM method, we conduct our experiments both on the sentences trained on the raw corpus and the sentences trained on the segmented corpus.

4.4 Results on Chinese-to-English Translation

30k Vocabulary Size. We list the BLEU scores of different translation granularities on 30k vocabulary in Table 2.

Table 2. Translation results (BLEU score) of 30k vocabulary for Chinese-to-English translation.

Segmentation (30k)	MT03(dev)	MT04	MT05	MT06	Ave
Word level	41.48	43.67	41.37	41.92	42.11
Character level	42.72	44.12	41.29	41.83	42.49
Hybrid word-characters level	43.24	45.18	**42.96**	42.89	43.57
BPE method	43.78	**45.47**	42.37	**43.37**	**43.75**
WPM method (raw)	41.96	43.38	40.84	40.98	41.79
WPM method	**44.12**	44.96	42.34	42.18	43.40

Row 1 is translation result of the state-of-the-art NMT system with word level. For the character level granularity (Row 2), the translation quality is higher than the word level by only 0.38 BLEU points. The last three lines in Table 2 is subword level translation granularity, which contains BPE method and WPM method. BPE method (Row 4) achieves the best translation performance, which gets an improvement of 1.64 BLEU points over the word level. As for the WPM method (Row 6), the gap between this method and BPE method is narrow. Moreover, hybrid word-character level model (Row 3) outperforms the word level by 1.46 BLEU points, and translation quality of this method is very close to the BPE method. Experiments show that hybrid word-character level granularity and BPE method of subword level granularity are our choices for translation granularity on Chinese-to-English translation task.

Comparison in Sentences of Different Lengths. We execute different translation granularities on the training corpus. To make a comparison, We randomly choose 10000 sentences. Table 3 show the average sentence length of different methods on all granularities.

A well-known flaw of NMT model is the inability to properly translate long sentences. However, most of translation granularities will go below the word level. Therefore, as shown in Table 3, we can get longer sentences than the word level. We wonder what the translation performance of different lengths on all translation granularities. We follow Bahdanau et al. [1] to group sentences of similar lengths together and compute a BLEU score per group, as demonstrated in Fig. 3.

Table 3. Sentence length of different translation granularities.

Language	Word	Character	Hybrid	BPE	WPM	WPM(raw)
Source (Chinese)	20.60	33.84	22.07	21.56	22.13	18.17
Target (English)	22.85	22.85	25.00	23.52	24.43	23.85

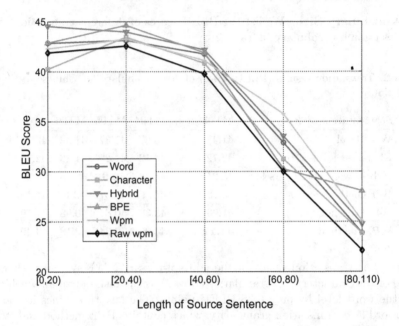

Fig. 3. Length analysis - translation qualities (BLEU score) of different lengths.

In order to make the comparison fair, length refer to the number of tokens split in word level. As above mentioned, hybrid word-character level model is one of suitable granularity choices for Chinese-to-English translation. We can find when the length of sentences is below 20, the translation result of this model outperforms the other models to a great extent. But with the length going up, the advantage over other models is diminishing. The character level granularity performs bad for the sentences whose length are below 20. We think the reason may be that when the sentences are short, the representation of sentence in character level cannot express the sentence meaning well. As for BPE method, we find a strange phenomenon. When the number of words in source sentence is from 60 to 80, the translation performance of BPE method is not so good. However, this method can achieve almost 3 BLEU points higher than next-best approach when the source sentence is longer than 80 words. As shown in Fig. 3, we can see WPM method does not perform well lower than 60 words in source language. But when the length of sentences is between 60 and 80, this method even outperforms the BPE method by up to 5.51 BLEU points. In this experiment, we conclude that subword are more effective than other models in handling long sentences.

15k Vocabulary Size. We concern what the translation result of different translation granularities on smaller vocabulary size. We also carry out the experiment on Chinese-to-English task of 15k vocabulary size.

Table 4. Translation results (BLEU score) of 15k vocabulary for Chinese-to-English translation.

Segmentation (15k)	MT03(dev)	MT04	MT05	MT06	Ave
Word level	39.03	42.42	38.84	39.58	39.97
Character level	42.60	43.60	40.85	41.29	42.09
Hybrid word-characters level	43.58	44.25	42.29	42.37	43.12
BPE method	**44.17**	44.89	42.79	**42.72**	43.64
WPM method (raw)	43.31	43.62	41.63	41.23	42.46
WPM method	44.03	**45.15**	**43.05**	42.63	**43.72**

Compared to 30k vocabulary size, the translation performance of word level (Row 1) on 15k vocabulary size reduce by 2.14 BLEU points. However, character level (Row 2) and hybrid word-character level (Row 3) achieves 42.09 and 43.12 BLEU points respectively, which is on par with quality of translation on 30k vocabulary. Both these two models exceed word level to a great extent. We infer the reason is that both character level and hybrid word-character level can represent source side and target side sentences better than the word level even if the vocabulary size is small. For subword model, translation performance of these methods remain almost the same as 30k vocabulary, which is beyond our imagination. We can find in Table 4, WPM method (Row 6) outperforms other models, and to our surprise, translation results of both WPM method and WPM methods with raw corpus (Row 5) obtain a higher BLEU points than 30k vocabulary size. We analyze the reason of this phenomenon is that the subword model is not constrained by the vocabulary size. Although the WPM method achieve the best results for the 15k vocabulary size, this method also belongs to subword level translation granularity. We can conclude that subword translation granularity is more suitable for Chinese-to-English translation task.

4.5 Results on English-to-Chinese Translation

We evaluate different translation granularities on the English-to-Chinese translation tasks, whose results are presented in Table 5. We find that hybrid word-character level (Row 3) granularity obtains significant accuracy improvements over word level and this granularity is also superior to other granularities on large-scale English-to-Chinese translation. BPE method (Row 4) in this task

Table 5. Translation results (BLEU score) for English-to-Chinese translation.

Segmentation (30k)	MT03(dev)	MT04	MT05	MT06	MT08	Ave
Word level	17.44	21.67	18.53	19.27	22.80	19.94
Character level	18.18	20.11	17.36	18.80	23.75	19.64
Hybrid word-characters level	19.81	23.28	20.99	**21.59**	**26.13**	**22.36**
BPE method	19.43	23.23	19.77	20.24	24.30	21.39
WPM method (raw)	18.66	21.19	18.34	18.43	19.06	19.14
WPM method	**20.78**	**24.05**	**21.07**	21.54	23.27	22.14

does not perform well as Chinese-to-English task, the translation quality of it is lower than hybrid word-character model by up to 0.97 BLEU points. However, another subword level translation granularity WPM method (Row 6) achieves 22.14 BLEU points, which is near the hybrid word-character level. Although the vocabulary of character level on Chinese side is only 7.2k, it can also obtain 19.64 BLEU points (Row 2), which is on par with translation performance of word level.

5   Related Work

The recently proposed neural machine translation has drawn more and more attention. Most of existing work in neural machine translation focus on handling rare words [12,15,19], integrating SMT strategies [6,21,25], designing the better framework [14,16] and addressing the low resource scenario [2,24].

As for strategies for dealing with rare and unknown words, Luong et al. [14] and Li et al. [12] propose simple alignment-based technique that can replace out-of-vocabulary words with similar words. Jean et al. [7] use a large vocabulary with a method based on importance sampling.

In addition, another direction to achieve rare words problem in NMT is changing the granularity of segmentation. Chung et al. [4] focus on handling translation at the level of characters without any word segmentation only on target side. Luong and Manning [13] propose a novel hybrid architecture that combines the strength of both word and character-based models. Sennrich et al. [19] use BPE method to encode rare and unknown words as sequences of subword units. Wu et al. [22] use both WPM method and hybrid word-character model in their online translation system. However, there is no study that shows which translation granularity is suitable for translation tasks involving Chinese language. Our goal in this work is to make an empirical comparison of different translation granularities for bidirectional Chinese-English translation tasks.

6   Conclusion

In this work, we provide an extensive comparison for translation granularities in Chinese-English NMT, such as word, character, subword and hybrid word-character. We have also discussed the advantages and disadvantages of various translation granularities in detail. The experiments demonstrate that the subword model best fits Chinese-to-English translation even with smaller vocabulary size, while the hybrid word-character approach obtains the highest performance on English-to-Chinese translation.

Acknowledgments. The research work has been funded by the Natural Science Foundation of China under Grant Nos. 61333018 and 61402478, and it is also supported by the Strategic Priority Research Program of the CAS under Grant No. XDB02070007.

References

1. Bahdanau, D., Cho, K., Bengio, Y.: Neural machine translation by jointly learning to align and translate. In: Proceedings of ICLR 2015 (2015)
2. Cheng, Y., Liu, Y., Yang, Q., Sun, M., Xu, W.: Joint training for pivot-based neural machine translation. arXiv preprint arXiv:1611.04928v2 (2017)
3. Chiang, D.: A hierarchical phrase-based model for statistical machine translation. In: Proceedings of ACL 2005 (2005)
4. Chung, J., Cho, K., Bengio, Y.: A character-level decoder without explicit segmentation for neural machine translation (2016)
5. Gage, P.: A New Algorithm for Data Compression. R & D Publications, Inc., Lawrence (1994)
6. He, W., He, Z., Wu, H., Wang, H.: Improved neural machine translation with SMT features. In: Proceedings of AAAI 2016 (2016)
7. Jean, S., Cho, K., Memisevic, R., Bengio, Y.: On using very large target vocabulary for neural machine translation. Computer Science (2014)
8. Junczys-Dowmunt, M., Dwojak, T., Hoang, H.: Is neural machine translation ready for deployment? A case study on 30 translation directions. In: Proceedings of IWSLT 2016 (2016)
9. Kalchbrenner, N., Blunsom, P.: Recurrent continuous translation models. In: Proceedings of EMNLP 2013 (2013)
10. Kingma, D.P., Ba, J.: Adam: A method for stochastic optimization. Computer Science (2014)
11. Koehn, P., Och, F.J., Marcu, D.: Statistical phrase-based translation. In: Proceedings of ACL-NAACL 2013 (2003)
12. Li, X., Zhang, J., Zong, C.: Towards zero unknown word in neural machine translation. In: Proceedings of IJCAI 2016 (2016)
13. Luong, M.T., Manning, C.D.: Achieving open vocabulary neural machine translation with hybrid word-character models (2016)
14. Luong, M.T., Pham, H., Manning, C.D.: Effective approaches to attention-based neural machine translation. In: Proceedings of EMNLP 2015 (2015)
15. Luong, M.T., Sutskever, I., Le, Q.V., Vinyals, O., Zaremba, W.: Addressing the rare word problem in neural machine translation. In: Proceedings of ACL 2015 (2015)
16. Meng, F., Lu, Z., Li, H., Liu, Q.: Interactive attention for neural machine translation. In: Proceedings of COLING 2016 (2016)
17. Papineni, K., Roukos, S., Ward, T., Zhu, W.: BLEU: a method for automatic evaluation of machine translation. In Proceedings of ACL 2002 (2002)

18. Schuster, M., Nakajima, K.: Japanese and Korean voice search, vol. 22, no. 10, pp. 5149–5152 (2012)
19. Sennrich, R., Haddow, B., Birch, A.: Neural machine translation of rare words with subword units. In: Proceedings of ACL 2016 (2016)
20. Sutskever, I., Vinyals, O., Le, Q.V.: Sequence to sequence learning with neural networks. In: Proceedings of NIPS 2014 (2014)
21. Wang, X., Lu, Z., Tu, Z., Li, H., Xiong, D., Zhang, M.: Neural machine translation advised by statistical machine translation. In: Proceedings of AAAI 2017 (2017)
22. Wu, Y., Schuster, M., Chen, Z., Le, Q.V., Mohammad Norouzi, et al.: Googles neural machine translation system: bridging the gap between human and machine translation. arXiv preprint arXiv:1609.08144 (2016)
23. Zhai, F., Zhang, J., Zhou, Y., Zong, C., et al.: Tree-based translation without using parse trees. In: Proceedings of COLING 2012 (2012)
24. Zhang, J., Zong, C.: Bridging neural machine translation and bilingual dictionaries. arXiv preprint arXiv:1610.07272 (2016)
25. Zhou, L., Hu, W., Zhang, J., Zong, C.: Neural system combination for machine translation. arXiv preprint arXiv:1704.06393 (2017)

An Unknown Word Processing Method in NMT by Integrating Syntactic Structure and Semantic Concept

Guoyi Miao[1,2], Jinan Xu[1(✉)], Yancui Li[2], Shaotong Li[1], and Yufeng Chen[1]

[1] School of Computer and Information Technology, Beijing Jiaotong University, Beijing, China
{gymiao,jaxu,shaotongli,chenyf}@bjtu.edu.cn
[2] Henan Institute of Science and Technology, Xinxiang, China
liyancui@hist.edu.cn

Abstract. The unknown words in neural machine translation (NMT) may undermine the integrity of sentence structure, increase ambiguity and have adverse effect on the translation. In order to solve this problem, we propose a method of processing unknown words in NMT based on integrating syntactic structure and semantic concept. Firstly, the semantic concept network is used to construct the set of in-vocabulary synonyms corresponding to the unknown words. Secondly, a semantic similarity calculation method based on the syntactic structure and semantic concept is proposed. The best substitute is selected from the set of in-vocabulary synonyms by calculating the semantic similarity between the unknown words and their candidate substitutes. English-Chinese translation experiments demonstrate that this method can maintain the semantic integrity of the source language sentences. Meanwhile, in performance, our proposed method can obtain an improvement by 2.9 BLEU points when compared with the conventional NMT method, and the method can also achieve an improvement by 0.95 BLEU points when compared with the traditional method of positioning the UNK character based on word alignment information.

Keywords: NMT · Unknown word · Syntactic structure · Semantic concept

1 Introduction

Although end-to-end NMT techniques [1, 2] have made a breakthrough in recent years, there still exist some problems difficult to solve, such as the unknown word problem. The unknown word will be replaced by the <UNK> character in the translation process. This brings some serious problems to NMT. First of all, <UNK> characters undermine the integrity of the structure and semantics of the source language sentence, and increase the ambiguity of the translation. Secondly, <UNK> characters lead to the result that the translation model cannot generate suitable translations.

Many researchers have proposed solutions for the problem of unknown words. For example, Xiaoqing Li et al. [6] have proposed a "replacement-translation-recovery" approach. Although this method can effectively find the similar words of the unknown

© Springer Nature Singapore Pte Ltd. 2017
D.F. Wong and D. Xiong (Eds.): CWMT 2017, CCIS 787, pp. 43–54, 2017.
https://doi.org/10.1007/978-981-10-7134-8_5

words, but this method does not fully consider whether the substitutes of the unknown words are suitable for the semantic context of the sentences. We analyze the following sentence in the source language.

He ate a round and red apple.
→   He ate <u>a round and red \<UNK\></u> .

The unknown word "apple" is represented as a \<UNK\> character, which is contained in the structure of a noun phrase {a round and red \<UNK\>}. The substitution of \<UNK\> is constrained by the semantics of the above phrase structure. If the substitute word of the unknown word deviates from the semantic environment of the new sentence, it will undermine the translation and decrease the quality of translation. Take the following sentences as examples:

(a) All income is subject to tax.
     Google translation: 所有收入均须<u>缴纳税款</u>。(Suoyou Shouru Junxu Jiaona Shuikuan.)
(b) All income is apt to tax.
     Google translation: 所有收入都很容易<u>征税</u>。(Suoyou Shouru Dou Hen Rongyi Zhengshui.)

In the sentence (a), if "subject" is an unknown word, it can be replaced by the synonym "apt". Comparing with the translation of the sentence (a), the translation of the sentence (b) is undermined in semantics. The "缴纳税款"(Jiaona Shuikuan) in the google translation of the sentence (a) becomes "征税" (Zhengshui) in the google translation of the sentence b). The main reason is that the word "apt" doesn't meet the semantic context of {is \<UNK\> to tax}. Therefore, in searching for the ideal substitute word of the unknown word, we should consider whether the substitute word meet the semantic context.

In this paper, we propose a new method to solve the problem of the unknown word. First of all, we use the semantic dictionary WordNet to search the synonyms of the unknown words in vocabulary. These synonyms are the candidate words to replace the unknown words. Then, we calculate the semantic similarity between the unknown word and the substitute word by using the semantic concept and syntactic structure, and choose the most suitable word to replace the unknown word. English-Chinese translation experiment shows that our method can effectively maintain the semantic integrity of the source language sentences and improve the quality of translations. Our proposed method can obtain an improvement by 2.9 BLEU points when compared with the conventional NMT method, and the method can also achieve an improvement by 0.95 BLEU points when compared with the traditional method of positioning the UNK character based on word alignment information.

The main contributions of this paper are as follows: First, we propose a new NMT unknown words processing method by integrating syntactic structure and semantic concept. And we show that this method does better in maintaining the semantic integrity of the source language sentence. Second, we introduce an effective semantic similarity calculation method to get the suitable substitute word for the unknown word.

The rest of this paper is structured as follows: Sect. 2 is about the related work. Section 3 introduces our proposed method of processing unknown words. Section 4 is about the experiments and the analysis of the experimental result. Section 5 is about the conclusion and future work.

2   Related Work

In order to solve the problem of the unknown words, many researchers have made great efforts. With the help of word alignment information in the traditional statistical Machine Translation, Luong et al. [3] located the UNK character in the target language by inserting position mark in the target language sentence, and after the translation, with the aid of locating information they processed the UNK character in the target language sentence by means of consulting the dictionary. Gulcehre et al. [4] embed a Copy Mode on the Neural Machine Translation Model, and in the decoding stage, the decoder can automatically make a choice on selecting words from the vocabulary to generate or selecting words from the source language sentence to copy. In order to ensure that the model training complexity does not increase significantly when large-scale vocabulary is used, Jean et al. [5] proposed a sampling method based on the importance. Li et al. [6] proposed a method of "replacement - translation - recovery". That is, in order to reduce the damage of the UNK character to the sentence structure and semantic integrity of the source language, synonyms in the set can be found out to replace the unknown words in accordance with the semantic similarity. The above Neural Machine Translation researches all take the word as the basic unit for modeling.

Compared with the word unit, fine-grain modeling, especially character modeling, has been studied extensively. Some researchers [7, 8] tried to solve the problem in translating the unknown words by fine-grain modeling, especially character modeling. In addition, Sennrich et al. [9] employed the Byte Pair Encoding algorithm to extract the subword unit and complete the split of the word; Luong and Manning [10] proposed a mixed character-word model to deal with the UNK character; Chung et al. [11] skipped the word unit, and employed Bi-Scale Recurrent Neural Network as a decoder to directly generate the character sequence in the target language.

3   Our Approach for Unknown Words

In general, our method of processing the unknown words in tested sentences is as follows: At first, we use the semantic network to filter and construct the set of candidate words in the set. Then, we make syntactic analysis on the tested sentences and extract the phrase information containing the unknown words. After that, we train a n-gram language model based on the source language. Combining the syntactic structure of the phrase and the semantic network WordNet, we use the language model to compute the semantic similarity between the unknown words and their substitute candidates, and select the most appropriate substitute with the highest similarity in semantics to replace the unknown word. The above steps are repeated until all the unknown words in the tested sentences are replaced, and then the tested sentences are decoded by the translation model to get the translation result. Since there is the translation of the substitutes in the translation result, it is necessary to replace the translation with the translation of the original unknown word. The implementation process of our method is shown in Fig. 1.

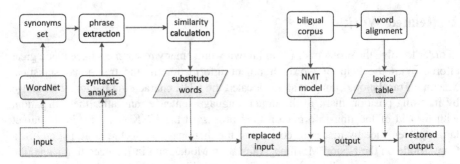

Fig. 1. Processing the unknown words. "Input" is the set of the tested sentences before decoding. "Output" is the translation result obtained by replacing and decoding the unknown word of "input". "Restored output" is the translation result obtained by replacing the translation of substitute with the translation of the unknown word.

3.1   Using the Semantic Concept Network

Considering that WordNet [15] has the advantage of making up data sparseness, we use it as a tool for selecting the substitutes to replace the unknown words. There are different semantic relationships between the semantic concepts in WordNet. Among them, the first two most commonly used relationships are synonymy and hyponymy. Specifically, WordNet3.0 contains 117659 concept nodes, with 82115 noun nodes, 13767 verb nodes, 18156 adjective nodes and 3621 adverb nodes. We screen out the synonym of each unknown word and construct the set of substitute candidates by using the lexical semantic network provided by WordNet3.0.

The proposed method is introduced as follows: First, in order to define the unknown word w and its part-of-speech POS_w, and initialize an empty set S_w as the set of substitute candidates, we find the semantic concept c of w whose part-of-speech is POS_w, and add all the synonyms of w in the concept node to S_w. Then, in order to offer enough optional synonyms to S_w, we use the relationship of hyponymy between the semantic concepts of WordNet. Starting from the concept node c, we add the synonym of c in the 3-layer superordinate semantic concept node to S_w and add the synonym of c in the 3-layer inferior semantic concept node to Sw. At last, we record w and its substitute candidate w_i respectively corresponding to the depth $d(w)$ and $d(w_i)$ of the semantic network root node R. In short, our method can offer abundant synonyms of w in the set of substitute candidates.

3.2   Phrase Analysis and Extraction

This section will make syntax analysis of the sentences to be decoded and extract all the phrases containing unknown words. The purpose is to determine whether the substitute candidates conform to the context of the phrase after they replace the unknown words. The phrase subtree obtained after the syntax analysis of the sentence is a relatively independent sub-component of the sentence. It may be a noun phrase or verb phrase, and even a noun phrase can be nested in a verb phrase. We define a phrase subtree structure, which consists of a five-tuple:

$$S = (\text{Line\_num, Name, Loc\_s, Loc\_e, Word\_num}) \tag{1}$$

In the structure, "Line_num" represents the line number of the sentence; "Name" represents the nature of the subtree; "Loc_s" represents the position of the subtree starting word in the sentence; "Loc_e" represents the position of the subtree closing words in the sentence; "Word_num" represents the number of word in the phrase. By using the five-tuple defined above, we extract the syntax analysis and the phrase subtree information of each sentence to be decoded, get the phrase information containing the unknown words and record them.

3.3   Calculating the Similarity

We divide the sentence by phrase structure and extract the phrase, and then set the phrase that the unknown word belongs to as a unit, with the substitute word to replace the unknown word, calculate the probability the phrase appears. This probability represents, to a large extent, the semantic similarity between the substitution word and its corresponding unknown word. Given the word pair (w_i', w_i), if w_i' is the substitute candidate word for the unknown word w_i, the phrase that the word w_i belongs to is described as $S = w_1 w_2 \cdots w_i \cdots w_l (l \geq 1)$, replace w_i with w_i' to get the phrase $phrase(w_i', w_i)$. We use a large-scale source language monolingual corpus to train a 3-gram language model in advance, using the language model to score the probability of $phrase(w_i', w_i)$ as follows. The score reflects the semantic similarity of the word pair to a great extent.

$$Score_{n-gram}(phrase(w_i', w_i)) = \sum_{j=1}^{l+1} p(w_j | w_{j-2}^{j-1}) \tag{2}$$

where w_i^j is described as $w_i \cdots w_j$.

In this paper, we use a simple method to calculate the similarity between the unknown word and its corresponding candidate substitution word in the semantic network. Assuming that the root node of the semantic hierarchical tree is R, $N(w_i')$ and $N(w_i)$ are the number of concept nodes that w_i' and w_i pass from the concept nodes they are located to the root node R. The larger the number of identical nodes passed by w_i' and w_i is, the more common their semantics are. The following formula represents the semantic coincidence between the two words w_i' and w_i. We use this semantic coincidence to represent the degree of similarity of the word *pair* (w_i', w_i) in the semantic network.

$$Score_{WordNet}(w_i', w_i) = \frac{|N(w_i') \cap N(w_i)|}{|N(w_i') \cup N(w_i)|} \tag{3}$$

The above formula can be calculated by $d(w_i')$ and $d(w_i)$ in Sect. 3.1.

Considering the similarity of the word *pair* (w_i', w_i) in the semantic network and the degree of adaptation in the context of context, we define the semantic similarity formula of the word *pair* (w_i', w_i) as:

$$Sim(w_i', w_i) = \frac{Score_{n-gram}(phrase(w_i', w_i)) + Score_{WordNet}(w_i', w_i)}{2} \tag{4}$$

The best substitution word is that with the highest similarity w_{best}, which is the synonym of the unknown word in semantics, and is suitable for the semantic context of the sentence in the maximum degree. w_{best} can be described as follows:

$$W_{best} = \arg\max_{w' \in S} sim(w', w) \tag{5}$$

3.4   Replacing the Unknown Word and Restoring the Translation Result

We replace all the unknown words with the substitutes, decode the input sentences with the translation model, and get the translation results. Because there are the translations of the substitutes of the unknown words in the translation results, it is necessary to replace the translations of the substitutes with the correct translations of the original unknown words.

We use GIZA++ [16] to train the training set to get a word alignment model and extract a bilingual dictionary containing all the words in the training corpus and their translations. This dictionary will help us to determine the alignment of the NMT source language and the target language. For the word t_i in the translation, if the alignment word s_j obtained based on the attention model by t_i is the substitute of the unknown word s_j', we use the bilingual dictionary to determine whether the alignment relation is right or not. If the translation pair (s_i, t_i) is in the bilingual dictionary, it shows that the alignment relation is correct, and t_i can be replaced by s_j'.

4   Experiments

We validate our method in English-Chinese translation task, and use BLEU4 [12] to evaluate the translation results.

4.1   Settings

The experimental data are derived from the evaluation corpus of CWMT2015. We selected 2 million parallel sentence pairs from the English and Chinese News Corpus provided by CWMT2015 as the training set, randomly selected non-overlapping 2000 sentence pairs from the 2 million parallel sentence pairs as the development set, and randomly selected 3000 sentence pairs as the test set. Meanwhile, 2 million English sentences in the training set were used to train the language model.

The syntax analysis tool we chose to use is Berkeley Parser, which is developed by the Natural Language Processing Group of Berkeley University. Berkeley Parser has a very stable performance of analytical accuracy on the WSJ test set (F = 90.1) [18], but in order to ensure the analysis accuracy, we manually checked the test corpus of 3,000 sentences after the analysis of Berkeley Parser.

4.2   Training Details

The super parameter settings used in our network are as follows: In experiments, we limited the size of both the source vocabulary and the target vocabulary to 30K. The hidden layer state dimensions of the source end and the target end are set to 512, and the word vector dimensions in the source end and the target end are set to 512. The parameters in the network are updated with the adadelta algorithm [13]. We set the batch size of the training set to 32 and set the Dropout rate [14] to 0.5.

4.3   Comparative Experiments

We have made a comparative experiment on different systems. Among them, Moses [17] uses hierarchical phrase model, and its target uses 3-gram language model. The RNNSearch system is our baseline system, which is an NMT system based on attention mechanism and do not make any unknown word processing. The PosUNK-based system uses the method proposed by Luong et al. [3] to locate <UNK> symbols in the target language by aligning information. Word2vec&lm system uses the method of "substitution-translation-restoration" proposed by Li et al. [6] to solve the problem of the unknown word. The WordNet&lm system uses WordNet to assist in filtering substitutes, and uses the usual similarity algorithm between words based on the 3-gram language model. The Subword-based system uses Byte Pair Encoding (BPE) algorithm [9] to extract the subword unit and complete the split of the word.

Based on the baseline system RNNSearch, WordNet-based system searches for the substitutes of the unknown words only by using WordNet. The calculation methods are shown in formula (3). WordNet&parsing is our best system, which integrates syntactic structure and semantic concept to operate with the unknown words. In order to analyze the different influence of noun phrase structure and verb phrase structure on the replacement of unknown words, we designed three subsystems VP-based, NP-based and VP+NP. Among them, VP-based only processes the unknown words contained in verbal phrases according to our method, and the rest unknown words are processed according to the method of WordNet&lm. NP-based only processes the unknown words contained in noun phrases according to our method, and the rest unknown words are processed according to the method of WordNet&lm. VP+NP is the integration of VP-based system and NP-based system.

4.4 Main Results

The main experimental results in Tables 1 and 2 show that our method is better than the baseline system (RNNSearch) because of the significant increase of 2.9 BLEU points in the mean value. Compared with the PosUNK-based system proposed by Luong et al. [3], our method has the upgrade of 0.95 BLEU value. Compared with the Word2-vec&lm system proposed by Li et al. [6], our method also has the improvement of 0.64 BLEU points. Our method has the weak promotion of the average 0.25 BLEU points in the VP-based subsystem and 0.47 BLEU points in the NP-based subsystem, which are better than that in WordNet&lm system. Although the BLEU value of our method is 0.32 points lower than that of subword-based method, our method does better in maintaining the semantic integrity of the source language sentence through empirical analysis.

Table 1. BLEU-4 scores (%) of different systems.

System	Dev	Tst	Average
Moses	28.38	26.88	27.63
RNNSearch	25.53	24.41	24.97
PosUNK-based	27.98	25.90	26.94
Word2vec&lm	28.49	26.01	27.25
WordNet&lm	28.15	26.33	27.24
Subword-based	28.94	27.47	28.21
WordNet-based (ours)	27.15	26.99	27.07
WordNet&parsing (our best)	**28.65**	**27.13**	**27.89**

Table 2. BLEU-4 scores (%) of our different subsystems.

System	Dev	Tst	Average
WordNet&lm	28.15	26.33	27.24
VP-only	27.87	27.11	27.49
NP-only	28.41	26.81	27.71
VP+NP	28.56	27.08	27.82

4.5 Analysis

In this section, we make specific analysis by comparing the methods of processing unknown words in different typical systems. Some translation examples are shown in Table 3.

Table 3. Translation examples

	Sentence
Example 1: The Source Sentence	The local officer whose partner **shot(UNK)** an Australian woman was "**startled (UNK)** by a loud sound" just before the incident, investigators say.
Reference	调查员说，一名当地警官的同伴**开枪**射杀了一名澳大利亚妇女，这名警官在事发前被一声巨响吓了**一跳**。
RNNSearch	当地官员的伙伴**<UNK >**一个澳大利亚女人是"**<UNK >**一个响亮的声音"，就在事发前，调查人员说。
PosUNK-based	调查人员说，一名当地官员的伙伴**拍摄**了一名澳大利亚女子，在事件发生前被"**震惊**了一声"。
Subword-based	The local officer whose partner shot an Australian woman was " **star@@ tled** by a loud sound " just before the incident , investigators say .
	调查人员说，在合伙人拍摄一名澳大利亚女性的当地官员在事件发生前**感到震惊**。
WordNet-based	A local officer whose partner **photograph** an Australian woman was " **scare** by a loud sound" just before the incident, investigators say.
	调查人员说，一名当地警官的伙伴**开枪**了一名澳大利亚女子，在事件发生前被"被一声响亮的声音吓了**一跳**"。
WordNet&parsing	A local officer whose partner **fired** an Australian woman was "**scare** by a loud sound" just before the incident, investigators say.
	调查人员说，一名当地官员的伙伴向一名澳大利亚女子身上**开枪**，在事发之前被"一声响亮的声音吓了**一跳**"。
Example 2: The Source Sentence	After he win the competition, his whole family live in **clover(UNK)** for the rest of their lives .
Reference	他赢得比赛后他全家从此过着**优裕的日子**。
RNNSearch	他赢得比赛后，他全家生活在**< UNK >**为他们的生活休息。
PosUNK-based	他赢得比赛后，他的全家过着余生，生活在三叶草中。
Subword-based	After he win the competition , his whole family live in **clo@@ ver** for the rest of their lives .
	在他赢得比赛后，他的整个家庭过着余生。
WordNet-based	After he win the competition, his whole family live in **trifolium** for the rest of their lives .
	在他赢得比赛后，他的整个家庭过着生活在三叶草里。
WordNet&parsing	After he win the competition, his whole family live in **comfort** for the rest of their lives .
	他赢得比赛后，全家人都过着舒适的三叶草。

In the above Examples, "shot", "startled" and "clover" are the unknown words in the source text. The performances of different methods are analyzed as follows:

First, the baseline system RNNSearch do not make any unknown word processing. It is obviously shown in the translation results that the <UNK> symbol in the source sentence seriously destroys the semantic integrity of the sentence, and leads to the problem of serious semantic deviation and words order confusion in translation.

Second, in the translation of PosUNK-based system, the Chinese term "拍摄" (Paishe) turns up due to incorrect alignment information.

Third, WordNet-based system uses the semantic concept to assist in screening out the synonyms of the unknown word to be the substitute. But whether the substitute is suitable for the semantic context or not isn't taken into consideration, so this method is not comprehensive enough. In Example 1, "shoot" is replaced by "photograph" in the WordNet-based system, and the semantics of the sentence is changed. Although the translation of "photograph" is corrected after the recovery operation, the word order of the translation is changed a lot, and this leads to a decline in the quality of translation.

Fourth, Subword-based system adapts byte pair encoding (BPE) for word segmentation and represents rare words as a sequence of subword units. And the experimental results show that it is effective in processing the unknown word problem. However, this method to a certain extent will undermine the semantic integrity of the sentence because of subword units, lead to missing translation, such as the translation results of subword-based system in Examples 1 and 2.

Fifth, WordNet&parsing is our best system. Our method can better maintain the integrity of the source language sentence and effectively reduce the adverse effects of the unknown word on the translation result. In Example 1, "shoot", the unknown word in the source text is a polysemous word. It has multiple synonyms. "Fire" is the most suitable synonym in the context, which can be concluded from the semantic context analysis of the phrase structure {<UNK> an Australian woman}. Therefore, "shot" is replaced by "fired", and the semantic integrity of the source text is maintained to the greatest extent, and good translation results are obtained.

Sixth, our method has some disadvantages, which cannot completely solve the problem of unknown words. WordNet&parsing has generated the wrong translation in Example 2. It can be found through analysis, the substitute "comfort" most suitable in semantics is screened out by our method which is based on the phrase structure {live in clover <UNK>}. But the translation of the substitute is replaced by the incorrect translation of the unknown word during the recovery stage. This phenomenon will be more obvious when the unknown word is polysemous. We still need further study to solve this problem.

5   Conclusion and Future Work

In this paper, we propose a new NMT unknown word processing method by integrating syntactic structure and semantic concept. And we introduce an effective semantic similarity calculation method to get the suitable substitute word for the unknown word. The English-Chinese translation experiment shows that our method can better maintain the integrity of the source language sentence and effectively reduce the adverse effects of the unknown word on the translation result. Meanwhile, this method increases the BLEU value by 2.9 points when compared with the conventional NMT method, and increases the BLEU value by 0.95 points when compared with the traditional method proposed by Luong et al. [3]. Although the BLEU value of our method is 0.32 points lower than that of subword-based method (BPE), our method is a new attempt based on syntactic structure and semantic concept and it is better to maintain the semantic integrity of the source language sentence. In the future work, we expect to have further research on selecting the better substitute to replace the unknown word from the deeper semantic context of the whole sentence.

Acknowledgments. The research work has been supported by the National Nature Science Foundation of China (Contract 61370130, 61473294 and 61502149), and Beijing Natural Science Foundation under Grant No. 4172047, and the Fundamental Research Funds for the Central Universities (2015JBM033), and the International Science and Technology Cooperation Program of China under grant No. 2014DFA11350.

References

1. Sutskever, I., Vinyals, O., Le, Q.V.: Sequence to sequence learning with neural networks. Adv. Neural. Inf. Process. Syst. **4**, 3104–3112 (2014)
2. Bahdanau, D., Cho, K., Bengio, Y.: Neural machine translation by jointly learning to align and translate. arXiv preprint arXiv:1409.0473 (2014)
3. Luong, M.T., Sutskever, I., Le, Q.V., et al.: Addressing the rare word problem in neural machine translation. Bull. Univ. Agricu. Sci. Vet. Med. Cluj-Napoca. Vet. Med. **27**(2), 82–86 (2014)
4. Gulcehre, C., Ahn, S., Nallapati, R., et al.: Pointing the unknown words. CoRR abs/1603.08148 (2016)
5. Jean, S., Cho, K., Memisevic, R., et al.: On using very large target vocabulary for neural machine translation. CoRR abs/1412.2007 (2014)
6. Li, X., Zhang, J., Zong, C.: Towards zero unknown word in neural machine translation. In: International Joint Conference on Artificial Intelligence, pp. 2852–2858. AAAI Press (2016)
7. Costa-Jussà, M.R., Fonollosa, J.A.R.: Character-based neural machine translation. CoRR abs/1603.00810 (2016)
8. Ling, W., Trancoso, I., Dyer, C., et al.: Character-based neural machine translation. arXiv preprint arXiv:1511.04586 (2015)
9. Sennrich, R., Haddow, B., Birch, A.: Neural machine translation of rare words with subword units. arXiv preprint arXiv:1508.07909 (2015)
10. Luong, M.T., Manning, C.D.: Achieving open vocabulary neural machine translation with hybrid word-character models. CoRR abs/1604.00788 (2016)
11. Chung, J., Cho, K., Bengio, Y.: A character-level decoder without explicit segmentation for neural machine translation. arXiv preprint arXiv:1603.06147 (2016)
12. Papineni, K., Roukos, S., Ward, T., et al.: BLEU: a method for automatic evaluation of machine translation. In: Meeting on Association for Computational Linguistics, pp. 311–318. Association for Computational Linguistics (2007)
13. Zeiler, M.D.: ADADELTA: an adaptive learning rate method. CoRR abs/1212.5701 (2012)
14. Srivastava, N., Hinton, G., Krizhevsky, A., et al.: Dropout: a simple way to prevent neural networks from overfitting. J. Mach. Learn. Res. **15**(1), 1929–1958 (2014)

15. Miller, G.A.: WordNet: a lexical database for english. Commun. ACM **38**(11), 39–41 (1995)
16. Och, F.J., Ney, H.: A systematic comparison of various statistical alignment models. Comput. Linguist. **29**(1), 19–51 (2003)
17. Collins, M., Koehn, P.: Clause restructuring for statistical machine translation. In: Meeting on Association for Computational Linguistics, pp. 531–540. Association for Computational Linguistics (2005)
18. Socher, R., Bauer, J., Manning, C.D., et al.: Parsing with compositional vector grammars. In: Meeting of the Association for Computational Linguistics, pp. 455–465 (2013)

RGraph: Generating Reference Graphs for Better Machine Translation Evaluation

Hongjie Ji, Shujian Huang$^{(\boxtimes)}$, Qi Hou, Cunyan Yin, and Jiajun Chen

State Key Laboratory for Novel Software Technology,
Nanjing University, Nanjing, China
{jihj,huangsj,houq,yincy,chenjj}@nlp.nju.edu.cn

Abstract. Statistical machine translation systems perform parameter learning (i.e. training) basing on automatic translation evaluation methods, which usually evaluate the translation quality according to one or more human-translated references. Although producing more references would improve the coverage of translation choices and lead to improved training performances, only several references are used due to the cost of human translation. In this paper, we propose automatic methods to explore the information among the limited references. By generating a reference graph (RGraph) from given references, we could automatically generate exponential number of references. These diverse references make it possible to better evaluate each individual translations, without using any other resources. Experiments showed that our RGraph could improve the evaluation performance and lead to better tuned machine translation systems. The method could be extended to improve the evaluation with single reference as well.

Keywords: Machine Translation Evaluation · Reference graph · Parameter learning · Evaluation metrics

1 Introduction

Statistical machine translation systems usually need to learn the system parameters using some training/tuning algorithms, such as Minimum Error Rate Training (MERT), Pair-wise Ranking Optimization (PRO) [16,26]. These training algorithms adjust the parameters so that the output of the system has a high translation quality. Because the translation quality is hard to evaluate, early attempts usually employ human to make the quality decision, which is very expensive and time-consuming [17]. Various metrics have been proposed to use automatical evaluation methods to replace human decisions, such as Word Error Rate (WER), BLEU and Translation Edit Rate (TER) [28,31]. These methods automatically evaluate similarity (or distance) between machine translation outputs and human-translated references.

Current evaluation methods can be roughly divided into two categories. The first category of methods are based on sentence-matching. These methods usually

© Springer Nature Singapore Pte Ltd. 2017
D.F. Wong and D. Xiong (Eds.): CWMT 2017, CCIS 787, pp. 55–67, 2017.
https://doi.org/10.1007/978-981-10-7134-8_6

compute an explicit one-to-one matching between words in the output sentence and a certain reference. The matching is then evaluated using metrics such as Levenshtein Distance [4,20,21,31,32] or matching precision and recall [4,11,12]. However, in order to generate an explicit matching, only one unique reference is considered. If there are multiple references, these methods need to select the one that is closest to the translation for the matching. This leads to potential problems when evaluating diverse translations. Because the same source language word or phrase could have multiple correct translations due to paraphrasing, the number of correct translations for a given source language sentence grows exponentially w.r.t the length of the sentence. When it is impossible to get an ideally "close" reference in one of the references, these methods may reach inaccurate quality decisions. In order to consider diversity in the evaluation process, external resources such as paraphrase tables or lexicon analysis are employed [1,4], but these resources may also bring in noises for the evaluation.

The second category of methods are segment-based. These approaches split the reference and the output into smaller segments, e.g. n-grams. The translation quality could be measured by the matching rate of segments, but without an explicit one-to-one matching [6,15,23,28]. Segment-based methods could naturally consider diverse translations, because the matching segments could come from any one of the references. However, because the matching of a translation segment could also come from any part of the reference, especially for those common function words, the quality measure could be less accurate. Besides, because the evaluation only focus on segments, the fluency of the whole sentence is less considered.

In this paper, we propose an evaluation approach that enjoys the benefits of both the above categories. By splitting the reference into segments and aligning them into a *Reference Graph*, we deeply explore the information inside the limited references and generate a compact representation that could represents exponentially many correct translations (Sect. 2). Selecting a path in the graph determines a certain reference translation; and metrics could be used to calculate distance between the output and the selected reference (Sect. 3). We also propose methods that explore monolingual resources to build the reference graph when only one reference is given (Sect. 2.3). Experiments demonstrate that our evaluation approach could achieve evaluation results better correlated to human decisions. Furthermore, tuning with reference graphs significantly improves the training performance of a large scale machine translation system, in both multiple reference and single reference settings (Sect. 4).

2   Constructing Reference Graph

The major problem of representing possible translations of a given source sentence by independent references is that it is impossible to enumerate all possible translations. So the evaluation would be unfair to the sentences with different word orders (shown in Fig. 1). Inspired by the practice of using confusion networks or lattices to represent translations from different systems in system

Ref1: as the stands of them are firm , the answer is clear .
Ref2: since their standces are really strong , the answer is very obvious .
Ref3: as their attitudes are very firm , the answer is obvious .
Ref4: since the stands of them are really strong , the answer is obvious .

(a)

Tran1: since their attitudes are firm , the answer is very clear .
Tran2: as since the stands are really very obvious ,

(b)

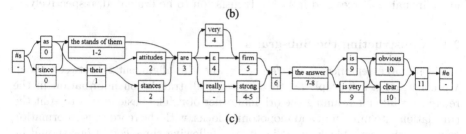

(c)

Fig. 1. The motivation example. (a) Shows the original 4 references; (b) shows two different translations: Tran1 is not close to any of the reference, which may lead to a lower score; Tran2 has several suspicious function words in incorrect places, which may lead to an overrate; (c) shows the RGraph built from these references, which may contain proper references for evaluating the quality of translations. In each vertex of the RGraph, upper cell presents the translations and the lower cell presents the indexes of the corresponding source part.

combination [5, 13, 14, 18, 19, 25], we propose to organize the references in a compact representation, named *Reference Graph* (RGraph) (shown in Fig. 1). With RGraph, the translation information inside the limited references can be better explored.

Different from the practice of confusion networks or lattices, which aligns all other translations to a selected back-bone translation and arrange them in the same order, we need to keep as many different word orders as possible to evaluate different translations. As a result, we choose to use the source sentence as the "back-bone" of the graph and align all possible translations in the reference to the source sentence. The alignment could be obtained using off-the-shelf alignment tools such as GIZA++ [27]. With the alignment, the construction of an RGraph is proceed in two steps: constructing sub-graph from every single reference, merging sub-graphs into the RGraph.

For convenience, we use the following notations throughout this paper. We denote the source sentence as $f = f_1, f_2, ..., f_l$, the reference as $r = r_1, r_2, ..., r_n$. The RGraph of f and its reference set R is a directed graph $D(f, R)$, or simply D, which consists of a vertex set V and an edge set E. Each vertex v in V represents a translation from source segment (f_i, f_j) to reference segment (r_p, r_q), including two pseudo vertices $\#_s$ and $\#_e$, which denotes the start and the end of a sentence. Because all references correspond to the same source sentence, we use source indexes instead of words in each node. So each vertex could be denoted as $\langle (i, j), (r_p, r_q) \rangle$. Each edge e in E connects two translation segments that are adjacent in the source side, e.g. from (i, k) to $(k + 1, j)$. A path p is made up of one or more vertexes connected by edges. p represents a source segment together with its translation, which is the concatenation of the source and target part of all vertexes in the path. Specifically, each path from $\#_s$ to $\#_e$ represents a possible translation of the whole sentence f. We use D_s, D_m and D_t to represent the directed graph constructed from a single reference, from monolingual resources and from the translation to be evaluated, respectively.

2.1 Constructing the Sub-graph

With a source sentence f, a reference r and the alignment A between them. We construct a sub-graph D_s that contains all translation information in the reference while maintaining the original order of r. The basic idea is to split the translation into minimum and monotonic blocks, with the reordering information covered inside each block. Specifically, the following three conditions should be satisfied: (1) no word in a block is aligned to words in other blocks; (2) the block is monotonic in both source and target side to its adjacent blocks; (3) the block is minimum, which means it could not be splitted into smaller blocks. An example of the block splitting results is in Fig. 2a.

The concept of blocks is the same as Mariño et al. [24], where similar bilingual n-grams are defined and referred to as *tuples*. With blocks, the whole sentence becomes a block sequence, which has the same order in both source and target side. This monotonic property leads to convenient algorithms for both constructing the graph and performing evaluation. The blocks are required to be minimum to cover the translation information at the finest level. Then larger segments of translation could be easily formed by merging consecutive blocks.

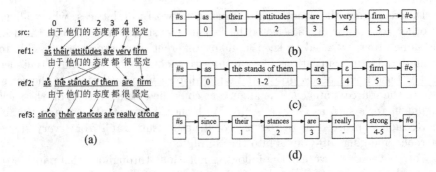

Fig. 2. An example of block splitting and sub-graph construction. (a) Shows blocks splitted according to the alignments for 3 references, respectively, where each underlined English phrase, together with its source counterpart forms a block; (b), (c) and (d) show sub-graphs constructed from ref1, ref2 and ref3, respectively, with one vertex to represent each block.

To construct the sub-graph, we generate a vertex for each block to represent the source segment (i, j), together with its target translation (r_p, r_q). These vertexes are then connected in their original order to form a directed sub-graph,

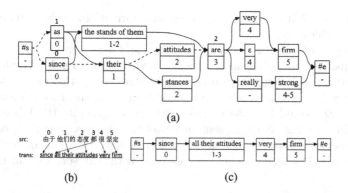

(a)

(b)

(c)

Fig. 3. An example of path-based graph search. The example searches in the RGraph in (a) for the closest reference for the translation in (b), which has a translation graph D_t shown in (c). We denote, for each vertex, the *minEdits* on top of it and the *minPath* to it by dashed lines. By far, the search proceeds at the *are* vertex. For the source span (1,3), the algorithm compares the following three paths "the stands of them are", "their attitudes are" and "their stances are", and selects the second one as the *minPath*. Further computation will be based on this selection.

which is the base of building a larger RGraph. Examples of the constructed sub-graphs are in Fig. 2.

Different from Mariño et al. [24] where NULL-aligned target words are appended to the previous words, we treat all NULL-aligned words as separate vertexes and insert them into the sub-graph as well. The ε vertex in Fig. 2c and the *really* vertex in Fig. 2d are examples in these cases.

2.2 Merging Sub-graphs

For multiple references, each reference will produce a sub-graph, these sub-graphs are then merged all together to form the RGraph. The merging process starts with an empty graph D and iteratively merges each sub-graph D_s into D. The merging first unions the vertex and edge set of the sub-graph into D, where vertexes covering the same source block with the same target translation are considered the same. Then new edges are added between adjacent vertexes in D and D_s. For example, between vertex $A\langle(i,k),(r_p,r_q)\rangle$ and $B\langle(k+1,j),(r_{p'},r_{q'})\rangle$ in D, an edge will be added from A to B if none of B's neighbors are NULL-aligned. It is easy to see that sub-graphs, which have just one path for the whole sentence, are simple versions of the RGraph. Figure 3a shows the result of merging three reference sub-graphs in Fig. 2.

2.3 Monolingual Extension of the Graph

In cases where there are only one single reference translation provided for each source sentence, it might be difficult to perform fair evaluations for diverse translation outputs. To solve the problem, we propose to enhance the single reference by building an RGraph using monolingual information, such as dictionaries, paraphrase tables, etc.

The single reference is firstly used to generate a sub-graph D_s as in previous sections. The monolingual resources are then used to generate alternative translations for each vertex or consecutive vertexes (i.e. paths) in D_s. We create new vertexes for these alternative translations and add them to an monolingual graph D_m. D_m could then be merged with D_s to generate the RGraph D as well, like in Sect. 2.2. Without sentence-level translations, it is not possible to add edges between vertexes in D_m. So we keep these vertexes unconnected. As a result, D_m could be seen as a special case of D with only vertexes but no edges.

3   Graph-Based Evaluation Metrics

Note that any given translation to be evaluated could also be transformed into a sub-graph (denoted by D_t) with the method described in Sect. 2.1. The alignment between the translation and the source sentence could be obtained by automatic alignments or as an extra output from the translation process. So the evaluation task now becomes evaluating the translation in D_t with RGraph D.

The evaluation could be executed in two steps. First, find the closest reference from the RGraph. Second, evaluate the translation according to the closest reference, with any metrics. The effectiveness of the two-step approach is evidenced by the experiment of Human-targeted Translation Error Rate, i.e. HTER [31], where human translator edits the reference so that it become closer to the given translation. Here we replace the human editing process with a graph matching process, which could be performed automatically without relying human editors.

To find the closest reference among the exponentially many possible references in the RGraph, we employ edit distance as the measure for closeness and perform a left-to-right search on the graph. Because the vertexes in D and D_t may cover different source segments, we use the paths as the basic search units.

The search process is similar to the Dijkstra's algorithm, except that our algorithm operates in the path level instead of vertex level. The distance is computed on-the-fly. As shown in Algorithm 1, for each vertex v, we compute the path ($minPath$) in D which ends in v, and has the number minimum of edits ($minEdits$). The algorithm starts from the path with a single node $\#_s$. It searches all possible paths according to the ending index of their source side block (using the priority queue, line 2), so that before calculating the edit distance for path p, all its prefix paths have been computed. Every time a path p fits a given path p_t in D_t suggests that the two paths cover the same source segment (line 7), thus their target sides could be measured by the edit distance algorithm (line 8). For any vertex v, only the path with minimum edits will be recorded for further extension (ensured by condition in line 9). Following computation would start from the successor of p, taking the previous path p and its minimum edits as basis (lines 12–13). If current path doesn't fit any path in D_t, all its successor will be enumerated to extend the path (lines 15–17). In worst cases, the extension lasts until the end word $\#_e$.

Algorithm 1. Path-based Graph Search Algorithm

Input: translation graph D_t with V_t, E_t and RGraph D with V, E
1: initialize each vertex $v \in V$ with $v.minEdits \leftarrow$ MAX, $v.minPath \leftarrow \emptyset$
2: priority queue of paths $pq \leftarrow \emptyset$ ▷ with the ending index of the source side block as the priority
3: path $start \leftarrow \#_s$, $start.edits \leftarrow 0$
4: $pq.$push($start$, 0)
5: **while** $pq \neq \emptyset$ **do**
6:     path $p \leftarrow pq.$pop(), $v \leftarrow$ the last vertex in p
7:     **if** p fits a path p_t in D_t **then**   ▷ p and p_t cover the same source segment
8:         $p.edits \leftarrow p.edits+$ editDistance(p, p_t)
9:         **if** $p.edits < v.minEdits$ **then**
10:             $v.minEdits \leftarrow p.edits$, $v.minPath \leftarrow p$
11:             **for all** successor $v' \in V$ of p **do**   ▷ finding shortest paths starting from v'
12:                 path $newp \leftarrow v'$, $newp.edits \leftarrow p.edits$, $newp.prePath \leftarrow p$
13:                 $pq.$push($newp$, $v'.end$)   ▷ v' covers source block ($start$, end)
14:     **else**   ▷ extending p with following vertexes to get a fit with D_t
15:         **for all** successor $v' \in V$ of p **do**
16:             path $newp \leftarrow p + v'$, $newp.edits \leftarrow p.edits$ ▷ $p + v'$ means appending v' to path p
17:             $pq.$push($newp$, $v'.end$)   ▷ v' covers source block ($start$, end)
Output: backtrace $\#_e.minPath$ will returns the path with minimum distance

Figure 3 shows an example of the path-based graph search algorithm. Note that, since the matching between the translation and the references are carried out for each source span, the spurious function word translations will be more carefully examined at this stage, compared previous segment-based approaches, such as BLEU.

4 Experiments

We perform experiments to compare the RGraph-based evaluation metrics we proposed against three standard and popular metrics: 4-gram case-insensitive BLEU, TER and Meteor [12,28,31]. Some statistics of the references before and after the RGraph extension are shown, including the correlation comparisons between the given metrics and human judgments. Then we present tuning comparisons including multiple and single reference cases.

4.1 Correlation with Human Judgments

For the correlation experiments, we use LDC2006T04 (MT03) as the experiment data, which contains 919 source language sentences and 4 references for each source sentence. Additionally, for each source sentence, 6 machine translation outputs are provided, together with their human evaluation scores, ranging from 1 to 5. We use the method in Sect. 2 to build RGraph from the given 4 references for each sentence. Table 1 shows the statistics after the RGraph extension. Besides 67 sentences (7%) which are not extended, more than 90% of the sentences get extra references generated. Among them, 263 sentences (29%) get more than 300 references. The average number of references in the RGraph reaches 125, which cover a significantly larger set of translation candidates compared to the original 4.

Table 1. #sents with different #refs after RGraph extension.

#refs	4	<10	<20	<300	>300	all
#sents	67	168	305	116	263	919
%		7%	18%	33%	13%	29%	100%

Table 3. Experiment data and statistics.

Data	Usage	Sentences
LDC	TM train	8,396,924
Gigaword	LM train	14,684,074
MT03	dev	919
MT02	test	878
MT04	test	1,788
MT05	test	1,082

Table 2. Comparison of correlations with human judgment.

Conditions	BLEU	TER	Meteor
w. 4-refs	0.4664	0.5066	0.4865
w. RGraph	**0.4739**	**0.5267**	**0.4876**

We compute the sentence-level evaluation score for each sentence in the dataset and calculate the correlations between these scores and the human evaluation results (Table 2). The first row shows the evaluation using BLEU, TER and Meteor on the original 4 references; the second row shows the results using the same three metrics but on the RGraph. The correlation efficient improves by a considerable margin for all three metrics, showing that evaluations using RGraph is closer to human judgment.

4.2   Tuning Experiments

To validate the influence of tuning metrics to the whole translation system, we perform tuning experiments on a large-scale machine translation task. Our translation system is an in-house implementation of the hierarchical phrase-based translation system [9], tuned with MERT [26]. The data used to train and test is listed in Table 3. The translation model (TM) of the system is trained on parallel sentences from LDC[1], which consists of 8.3 million of sentence pairs. The Chinese side of the corpora is word segmented using ICTCLAS[2]. We train a 5-gram language model (LM) with MKN smoothing [8], on Xinhua portion of Gigaword. We use multi-reference data MT03 as the development (dev) data, MT02, MT04 and MT05 as the test data. These data are mainly in the same genre, avoiding the extra consideration of domain adaptation. All the reported results are the average of three independent MERT runs with random starting points [10].

We tune the systems with original BLEU and BLEU with the RGraph extension (denoted as GBLEU), respectively, and evaluate the translation result using all previous mentioned metrics (Table 4). Different rows show the evaluation results in different metrics on all three test sets and their average. The left and right half of the table present the system tuned with BLEU and GBLEU, respectively. It could be easily seen that tuning with GBLEU achieves superior performances in all the listed metrics.

---

[1] including LDC2002E18, LDC2003E14, LDC2004E12, LDC2004T08, LDC2005T10, LDC2007T09.

[2] http://ictclas.nlpir.org/.

Table 4. Comparisons between tuning with BLEU and GBLEU. "ave" denotes the average results across three testsets. "Δ-ave" denotes the difference of scores in each evaluation metric and † indicates statistically significant difference ($p < 0.01$) between systems tuned with GBLEU and BLEU, respectively.

	Tuned with BLEU				Tuned with GBLEU				
Evaluate	MT02	MT04	MT05	ave	MT02	MT04	MT05	ave	Δ-ave
BLEU	37.71	37.28	36.65	37.21	37.77	37.49	36.69	37.31	**+0.10**
1-TER	43.96	43.81	44.07	43.95	44.92†	44.66†	45.04†	44.87	**+0.93**
Meteor	32.88	32.56	33.03	32.82	33.04†	32.70†	33.33†	33.03	**+0.22**
GBLEU	26.90	27.01	28.22	27.38	27.73	27.69	28.95	28.13	**+0.75**
1-GTER	45.57	45.66	45.75	45.66	47.28	47.30	47.36	47.31	**+1.65**
GMeteor	32.83	32.38	32.63	32.61	33.08	32.68	33.06	32.94	**+0.33**

Despite the improvement on RGraph-based metrics, it is interesting to notice that the score increases on all the original metrics computed on the 4 references (by +0.1 in BLEU, +0.93 in TER and +0.22 in Meteor). This improvement could only be explained by the improvement of overall system performance. This result demonstrate that the improvement in evaluation metrics does lead to a stronger statistical system, which may encourage further investigations in the research of evaluation metrics.

4.3   Experiments with a Single Reference

To generate RGraphs from single references, we employ the paraphrase table from Pavlick et al. [29], named PPDB. We use the small size English paraphrase table in PPDB, which has a higher precision, and only use pairs labeled as 'Equivalence' to reduce noisy translations. We construct the monolingual graph D_m using paraphrases for sub-paths that contain less than 3 vertexes, and merge D_m to the D_s of the single reference. Similar with previous experiments, we use BLEU and GBLEU to tune our systems on MT03. The systems are tuned with each reference, and with the monolingual extension of each reference, respectively. The average results are listed in Table 5. Similar with the results in the multi-reference case, the system tuned with GBLEU achieves better results in most of the metrics (by +0.49 in BLEU, +1.40 in TER, etc.). We notice that the results decrease in Meteor. One possible explanation is that the paraphrase matching used by Meteor plays a similar role as our monolingual extension. However, when multiple references is given, our method do explore the references better, even when evaluated with Meteor, as shown in Table 4.

Because systems tuned with different references vary in performance, we further examine those differences (shown in Fig. 4). The error bar shows the maximum and minimum score in the systems tuned by the each single reference. Despite the higher average scores, it is easy to see that systems tuned with GBLEU has a much smaller variance in both BLEU and GBLEU scores,

Table 5. Comparisons between tuning with BLEU and GBLEU on single references. Each score is the results averaged over the system tuned with each of the 4 references. "ave" denotes the average results across the three testsets. "Δ-ave" denotes the difference of scores in each evaluation metric and † indicates statistically significant difference ($p < 0.01$) between systems tuned with GBLEU and BLEU, respectively.

	Tuned with BLEU				Tuned with GBLEU				
Evaluate	MT02	MT04	MT05	ave	MT02	MT04	MT05	ave	Δ-ave
BLEU	36.45	36.36	35.94	36.26	36.94	36.89	36.43	36.75	**+0.49**
1-TER	41.01	41.23	41.54	41.26	42.43†	42.54†	42.99†	42.66	**+1.40**
Meteor	33.34	33.02	33.48	33.28	33.10	32.79	33.25	33.05	−0.23
GBLEU	25.81	25.94	26.97	26.24	26.40	26.47	27.62	26.83	**+0.59**
1-GTER	42.61	43.02	42.80	42.81	44.29	44.53	44.55	44.46	**+1.65**
GMeteor	33.16	32.79	33.00	32.98	32.98	32.63	32.85	32.82	−0.16

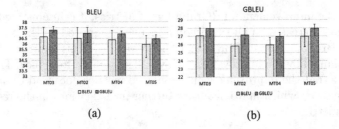

(a)   (b)

Fig. 4. The BLEU(a) and GBLEU(b) scores of the single reference experiments. The white and shaded pillars indicates system scores (averaged over 4 references) tuned by BLEU and GBLEU, respectively. The error bars depict the minimum and maximum scores tuned on each single reference.

compared to systems tuned with BLEU. This result suggests that the tuning result with single reference may highly depend on the quality of the reference. Using RGraph as the tuning metric helps to reduce this influence and leads to generally more stable results.

5 Related Work

There are several related works focusing on other properties or conditions of the references. Snover et al. [31] proposed to use human edited reference which could achieve evaluation results better correlated with human decisions. Our method tries to automatically generate close references instead. Qin and Specia [30] proposed an approach to explore the information among references. Their work mainly focuses on selecting essential words or expressions using recurring information among references; while our work is to increase the coverage of diverse translations. Albrecht and Hwa [2,3] proposed to use translations from other machine translation systems or large monolingual corpora or tree banks as pseudo references instead of references. They focused on the problem where no human translations are available.

There are other researches proposing tuning metrics for machine translation. Chen et al. [7] proposed a metric named PORT, which combines precision, recall and an ordering metric for better tuning in MT systems. Li et al. [22] used a dependency-based MT evaluation metric RED for Tuning. These methods could also be applied in our RGraph approach. With a closer reference generated by RGraph, it is possible to achieve even better results with these improved tuning methods.

6   Conclusion

This paper aims at properly evaluating the translation quality of machine translation outputs. This is a special problem because different from traditional tasks such as pos-tagging and parsing, there is more than one correct answer in machine translation tasks. It could be an important issue to consider for tasks which have similar properties, such as text summarization, language generation and image caption.

We notice that improving the diversity of the references is important for the evaluation task as well as the tuning of the system. For statistical machine translation systems such as the hierarchical phrase based systems, we have demonstrated that better evaluation metrics do lead to better trained system. It is now interesting to investigate the translation diversity in other architectures such as neural machine translation systems.

We use off-the-shelf alignment tools to obtain the alignment between the references and the source sentence, which is quite noisy for some sentences. We believe that better alignments could lead to even better evaluation performance.

Acknowledgments. This work is supported by the National Science Foundation of China (Nos. 61672277, 61772261), the Jiangsu Research Foundation for Basic Research (No. BK20170074).

References

1. Agarwal, A., Lavie, A.: Meteor, M-BLEU and M-TER: evaluation metrics for high-correlation with human rankings of machine translation output. In: Proceedings of the Third Workshop on Statistical Machine Translation, Columbus, Ohio, pp. 115–118. Association for Computational Linguistics (2008)
2. Albrecht, J., Hwa, R.: Regression for sentence-level MT evaluation with pseudo references. In: Proceedings of the 45th Annual Meeting of the Association of Computational Linguistics, Prague, Czech Republic, pp. 296–303. Association for Computational Linguistics (2007)
3. Albrecht, J., Hwa, R.: The role of pseudo references in MT evaluation. In: Proceedings of the Third Workshop on Statistical Machine Translation, Columbus, Ohio, pp. 187–190. Association for Computational Linguistics, June 2008

4. Banerjee, S., Lavie, A.: METEOR: an automatic metric for MT evaluation with improved correlation with human judgments. In: Proceedings of the ACL Workshop on Intrinsic and Extrinsic Evaluation Measures for Machine Translation and/or Summarization, Ann Arbor, Michigan, pp. 65–72. Association for Computational Linguistics (2005)
5. Bangalore, B., Bordel, G., Riccardi, G.: Computing consensus translation from multiple machine translation systems. In: 2001 IEEE Workshop on Automatic Speech Recognition and Understanding, ASRU 2001, pp. 351–354 (2001)
6. Chan, Y.S., Ng, H.T.: MaxSim: performance and effects of translation fluency. Mach. Transl. **23**(2–3), 157–168 (2009)
7. Chen, B., Kuhn, R., Larkin, S.: Port: a precision-order-recall MT evaluation metric for tuning. In: Proceedings of the 50th Annual Meeting of the Association for Computational Linguistics, Long Papers, vol. 1, pp. 930–939. Association for Computational Linguistics (2012)
8. Chen, S.F., Goodman, J.: An empirical study of smoothing techniques for language modeling. In: Proceedings of the 34th Annual Meeting of the Association for Computational Linguistics, Santa Cruz, California, USA, pp. 310–318. Association for Computational Linguistics (1996)
9. Chiang, D.: A hierarchical phrase-based model for statistical machine translation. In: Proceedings of the 43rd Annual Meeting of the Association for Computational Linguistics, Ann Arbor, Michigan, pp. 263–270. Association for Computational Linguistics (2005)
10. Clark, J.H., Dyer, C., Lavie, A., Smith, N.A.: Better hypothesis testing for statistical machine translation: controlling for optimizer instability. In: Proceedings of the 49th Annual Meeting of the Association for Computational Linguistics: Human Language Technologies, Portland, Oregon, USA, pp. 176–181. Association for Computational Linguistics (2011)
11. Denkowski, M., Lavie, A.: Meteor-next and the meteor paraphrase tables: improved evaluation support for five target languages. In: Proceedings of the Joint Fifth Workshop on Statistical Machine Translation and MetricsMATR, Uppsala, Sweden, pp. 339–342. Association for Computational Linguistics (2010)
12. Denkowski, M., Lavie, A.: Meteor universal: language specific translation evaluation for any target language. In: Proceedings of the Ninth Workshop on Statistical Machine Translation, Baltimore, Maryland, USA, pp. 376–380. Association for Computational Linguistics (2014)
13. Du, J., Jiang, J., Way, A.: Facilitating translation using source language paraphrase lattices. In: Proceedings of the 2010 Conference on Empirical Methods in Natural Language Processing, Cambridge, MA, pp. 420–429. Association for Computational Linguistics (2010)
14. Feng, Y., Liu, Y., Mi, H., Liu, Q., Lü, Y.: Lattice-based system combination for statistical machine translation. In: Proceedings of the 2009 Conference on Empirical Methods in Natural Language Processing, Singapore, pp. 1105–1113. Association for Computational Linguistics (2009)
15. Han, A.L.F., Wong, D.F., Chao, L.S.: LEPOR: a robust evaluation metric for machine translation with augmented factors, pp. 441–450 (2012)
16. Hopkins, M., May, J.: Tuning as ranking. In: Proceedings of the 2011 Conference on Empirical Methods in Natural Language Processing, Edinburgh, Scotland, UK, pp. 1352–1362. Association for Computational Linguistics (2011)
17. Hovy, E.: Toward finely differentiated evaluation metrics for machine translation. In: Proceedings of the EAGLES Workshop on Standards and Evaluation, pp. 127–133 (1999)

18. Jayaraman, S., Lavie, A.: Multi-engine machine translation guided by explicit word matching. In: Proceedings of the ACL Interactive Poster and Demonstration Sessions, Ann Arbor, Michigan, pp. 101–104. Association for Computational Linguistics (2005)

19. Jiang, J., Du, J., Way, A.: Incorporating source-language paraphrases into phrase-based SMT with confusion networks. In: Proceedings of Fifth Workshop on Syntax, Semantics and Structure in Statistical Translation, Portland, Oregon, USA, pp. 31–40. Association for Computational Linguistics (2011)

20. Leusch, G., Ueffing, N., Ney, H.: A novel string-to-string distance measure with applications to machine translation evaluation. In: MT Summit IX, New Orleans, LA, pp. 240–247 (2003)

21. Leusch, G., Ueffing, N., Ney, H.: CDER: efficient MT evaluation using block movements. In: 11th Conference of the European Chapter of the Association for Computational Linguistics (2006)

22. Li, L., Yu, H., Liu, Q.: MT tuning on RED: a dependency-based evaluation metric. In: Proceedings of the Tenth Workshop on Statistical Machine Translation, Lisbon, Portugal, pp. 428–433. Association for Computational Linguistics (2015)

23. Liu, C., Dahlmeier, D., Ng, H.T.: TESLA: translation evaluation of sentences with linear-programming-based analysis. In: Proceedings of the Joint Fifth Workshop on Statistical Machine Translation and MetricsMATR, Uppsala, Sweden, pp. 354–359. Association for Computational Linguistics (2010)

24. Mariño, J.B., Banchs, R.E., Crego, J.M., de Gispert, A., Lambert, P., Fonollosa, J.A.R., Costa-jussà, M.R.: N-gram-based machine translation. Comput. Linguist. **32**(4), 527–549 (2006)

25. Matusov, E., Ueffing, N., Ney, H.: Computing consensus translation for multiple machine translation systems using enhanced hypothesis alignment. In: 11th Conference of the European Chapter of the Association for Computational Linguistics (2006)

26. Och, F.J.: Minimum error rate training in statistical machine translation. In: Proceedings of ACL 2003, Sapporo, Japan, pp. 160–167. Association for Computational Linguistics (2003)

27. Och, F.J., Ney, H.: A systematic comparison of various statistical alignment models. Comput. Linguist. **29**(1), 19–51 (2003)

28. Papineni, K., Roukos, S., Ward, T., Zhu, W.J.: BLEU: a method for automatic evaluation of machine translation. In: Proceedings of ACL 2002, Philadelphia, Pennsylvania, USA, pp. 311–318. Association for Computational Linguistics (2002)

29. Pavlick, E., Rastogi, P., Ganitkevitch, J., Van Durme, B., Callison-Burch, C.: PPDB 2.0: Better paraphrase ranking, fine-grained entailment relations, word embeddings, and style classification. In: Proceedings of the 53rd Annual Meeting of the Association for Computational Linguistics and the 7th International Joint Conference on Natural Language Processing, Beijing, China, pp. 425–430. Association for Computational Linguistics (2015). http://www.aclweb.org/anthology/P15-2070

30. Qin, Y., Specia, L.: Truly exploring multiple references for machine translation evaluation. In: 18th Annual Conference of the European Association for Machine Translation, EAMT, Antalya, Turkey (2015)

31. Snover, M., Dorr, B.J., Schwartz, R.: A study of translation edit rate with targeted human annotation. In: Proceedings of AMTA (2006)

32. Snover, M.G., Madnani, N., Dorr, B., Schwartz, R.: TER-Plus: paraphrase, semantic, and alignment enhancements to translation edit rate. Mach. Transl. **23**(2), 117–127 (2009)

ENTF: An Entropy-Based MT Evaluation Metric

Hui Yu[1], Weizhi Xu[1], Shouxun Lin[2], and Qun Liu[2,3]($\boxtimes$)

[1] School of Management Science and Engineering, Shandong Normal University,
Jinan, China
{huiyu0117,xuweizhi}@sdnu.edu.cn
[2] Key Laboratory of Intelligent Information Processing,
Institute of Computing Technology, Chinese Academy of Sciences, Beijing, China
sxlin@ict.ac.cn
[3] ADAPT Centre, School of Computing, Dublin City University, Dublin, Ireland
qun.liu@dcu.ie

Abstract. The widely-used automatic evaluation metrics cannot adequately reflect the fluency of the translations. The n-gram-based metrics, like BLEU, limit the maximum length of matched fragments to n and cannot catch the matched fragments longer than n, so they can only reflect the fluency indirectly. METEOR, which is not limited by n-gram, uses the number of matched chunks but it does not consider the length of each chunk. In this paper, we propose an entropy-based metric (ENTF), which can sufficiently reflect the fluency of translations through the distribution of matched words. To evaluate the accuracy, we also introduce the unigram F-score into the new metric. Experiment shows that ENTF obtains state-of-the-art performance on system level, and is comparable with METEOR on sentence level on into English direction on WMT 2012, WMT 2013 and WMT 2014.

Keywords: Automatic evaluation metric · Machine translation · Entropy-based metric

1 Introduction

Automatic machine translation (MT) evaluation plays an important role in the evolution of MT. It not only evaluates the performance of MT systems, but also provides guidance for the improvement of MT systems [15].

The automatic MT evaluation metrics can be classified into three categories: lexicon-based methods [2,3,10,17,21], syntax-based methods [1,11,14,16,22] and semantic-based methods [12], according to the employed information type. Most of lexicon-based metrics obtain similarity between references and hypotheses based on n-gram, such as BLEU [17] and NIST [5]. BLEU obtains scores by a geometric mean of the n-gram precisions and a length-based penalty. NIST is closely related to BLEU but uses the arithmetic mean instead of geometric mean. For these metrics, the maximum length of matched fragments is limited to n, so they cannot catch the matched fragments longer than n. Some metrics which are not

© Springer Nature Singapore Pte Ltd. 2017
D.F. Wong and D. Xiong (Eds.): CWMT 2017, CCIS 787, pp. 68–77, 2017.
https://doi.org/10.1007/978-981-10-7134-8_7

limited by n-grams relieve this problem, such as METEOR [10]. METEOR uses F-score of unigrams and a penalty. The penalty in METEOR is related to the number of matched chunks[1]. When the number of chunks in two sentence are same, METEOR doesn't distinguish them. The syntax-based metrics obtain the similarity by comparing the syntactic structures of two trees, and they cannot reflect the fluency directly. Semantic-based metrics, such as MEANT [12] which uses semantic role labeling (SRL) to match the predicate and arguments, mainly obtain the semantic information and do not consider the fluency.

In this paper, we propose an entropy-based method, which can sufficiently reflect the fluency of translations through the distribution of matched words. To evaluate the accuracy, we also introduce the unigram F-score into the new metric. Experiment shows that, on into English direction, ENTF obtains state-of-the-art performance on system level and is comparable with METEOR on sentence level on WMT 2012, WMT 2013 and WMT 2014.

2 ENTF: An Entropy-Based MT Evaluation Metric

The two important factors for a good MT evaluation metric are fluency and accuracy. In this section, We introduce an entropy-based MT evaluation metric which reflects fluency through an **ENT**ropy-based method and reflects accuracy through unigram **F**-score, so we name it as ENTF.

2.1 ENT: Entropy-Based Fluency Evaluation

Entropy is a measure of the uncertainty in a random variable. Shannon denoted the entropy H of a discrete random variable x with possible values $x_1, x_2, \ldots, x_n$. The entropy is defined as Formula (1) [20].

$$H(X) = -\sum_{i=1}^{n} P(x_i) log_2 P(x_i) \qquad (1)$$

$P(x_i)$ is the probability of x_i showing up in the stream of characters. The more decentralized of the values $x_1, x_2, \ldots, x_n$, the higher of the entropy H(X). So the entropy can reflect the distribution of the values of variable x.

In the automatic evaluation of machine translation, entropy can reflect the distribution of matched words. A lower entropy corresponds to a more concentrate distribution of matched words which represents a more fluent hypothesis. On the contrary, a higher entropy corresponds to a more disperse distribution of matched words, which represents a less fluent hypothesis. So the entropy-based method can reflect the fluency of translations sufficiently by the distribution of the words.

An example (a reference and three hypotheses) is shown in Table 1. In the example, the matched words are in bold. hyp1, hyp2 and hyp3 can all match four

---

[1] The words in each chunk are in adjacent positions in the hypothesis, and are also mapped to unigrams that are in adjacent positions in the reference.

Table 1. An example: one reference and three hypotheses.

ref:	There are books on the desk
hyp1:	**There are books** in that **desk**
hyp2:	**There are** table **on the** book
hyp3:	**There are** table **on** book **the**

words, but the distribution of the four words are different. The matched words are in two chunks for hyp1 and hyp2, and three chunks for hyp3. A smaller number of chunks represents a more concentrated distribution of the matched words, and corresponds to a more fluent hypothesis. From this point of view, hyp1 and hyp2 are better than hyp3. hyp1 has the same number of chunks as hyp2 but the number of the matched words in the two chunks is (3, 1) for hyp1 and (2, 2) for hyp2. hyp1 is considered to be more fluent than hyp2.

The details of the ENT are represented in the following four steps.

- obtain the alignment between reference and hypothesis
  The alignment is derived using Meteor Aligner[2]. Some automatic evaluation metrics can only find the exact match between the reference and the translation, and the information provided by the limited number of references is not sufficient. Some evaluation metrics, such as TERp and METOER, introduce extra resources to expand the reference information. We also introduce some extra resources, such as stem [19], synonym (Wordnet[3]) and paraphrase. When obtaining the alignment using METEOR Aligner, all of the four match modules (exact, stem, synonym and paraphrase) in METEOR are considered.
- classify the matched words into chunks using the alignment
  The matched words in the alignment are considered to be in a chunk if they are continuous and appear in the same order in both reference and hypothesis.
- calculate the entropy of chunks
  the entropy of chunks is calculated using Formula (2).

$$H = -\sum_{i=1}^{c} \frac{l_i}{L} log(\frac{l_i}{L}) \tag{2}$$

l_i is the length of the ith chunk. c is the number of the chunks. L is the total number of the matched words.
- obtain the final score of ENT
  - Length penalty
    The length penalty is calculated by Formula (3). l_h is the length of hypothesis. l_r is the length of reference.

$$LP = 1.1^{|\frac{l_h}{l_r}-1|} \tag{3}$$

---

[2] http://www.cs.cmu.edu/~alavie/METEOR/.
[3] http://wordnet.princeton.edu/.

– Normalization

To obtain a score within scope (0,1), an exponential function is used as formula (4). We use $-H$ instead of H in the formula to ensure that a higher score of ENT represents a more fluent translation. The final score of ENT is achieved by Formula (4).

$$ENT = \alpha^{-H \times LP}, \quad \alpha \in (1, 1.5) \tag{4}$$

Using Formula (4), the scores of the example in Table 1 can be obtained as follows.

$$LP_{hyp1} = LP_{hyp2} = LP_{hyp3} = 1.1^{|\frac{6}{6}-1|} = 1$$

$$ENT_{hyp1} = \alpha^{-(-(\frac{3}{4}log\frac{3}{4}+\frac{1}{4}log\frac{1}{4})) \times 1} \approx \alpha^{-0.24}$$

$$ENT_{hyp2} = \alpha^{-(-(\frac{2}{4}log\frac{2}{4}+\frac{2}{4}log\frac{2}{4})) \times 1} \approx \alpha^{-0.30}$$

$$ENT_{hyp3} = \alpha^{-(-(\frac{2}{4}log\frac{2}{4}+2\times\frac{1}{4}log\frac{1}{4})) \times 1} \approx \alpha^{-0.45}$$

We can see that $ENT_{hyp1} > ENT_{hyp2} > ENT_{hyp3}$. Accordingly, the quality of hyp1 is obviously better than hyp2, and hyp2 is better than hyp3. So the entropy-based fluency evaluation method can distinct these situations well.

2.2 F-Score: Accuracy Evaluation

Except fluency, another important factor for a good MT evaluation metric is accuracy. So we introduce the unigram F-score into the new metric to evaluate the accuracy. The words within a sentence can be classified into content words and function words. The effects of the two kinds of words are different and they should not have the same matching score, so we introduce a parameter w_f to distinguish them. We have obtained the alignment in the entropy-based fluency evaluation so the alignment can be directly used in calculating F-score. Every matched word was labeled by the match module, such as *exact, stem, synonym* and *paraphrase*. the precision P and recall R can be calculated by Formulas (5) and (6) separately.

$$P = \frac{\sum_i m_i \cdot (w_f \cdot f_h(i) + (1-w_f) \cdot c_h(i))}{w_f \cdot num_c(h) + (1-w_f) \cdot num_f(h)} \tag{5}$$

$$R = \frac{\sum_i m_i \cdot (w_f \cdot f_r(i) + (1-w_f) \cdot c_r(i))}{w_f \cdot num_c(r) + (1-w_f) \cdot num_f(r)} \tag{6}$$

In Formula (5), i is the ith word in the matched unigram, $0 < i \le n$, and n is the number of the matched unigrams. m_i is the match weight of the ith matched word. w_f is the weight of function words. $num_f(h)$ is the number of function words in the hypothesis, and $num_c(h)$ is the number of content words in the hypothesis. $f_h(i)$ represents whether the ith matched unigram in hypothesis is function word.

$$f_h(i) = \begin{cases} 1 & \text{if function word} \\ 0 & \text{if not function word} \end{cases}$$

$c_h(i)$ represent whether the ith matched unigram in hypothesis is content word.

$$c_h(i) = \begin{cases} 1 & if\ content\ word \\ 0 & if\ not\ content\ word \end{cases}$$

In Formula (6), i, m_i and w_f have the same meanings as those in Formula (5). $num_f(r)$ and $num_c(r)$ are the number of function words and content words in reference separately. $f_r(i)$ represents whether the ith matched word in reference is function word.

$$f_r(i) = \begin{cases} 1 & if\ function\ word \\ 0 & if\ not\ function\ word \end{cases}$$

$c_r(i)$ represent whether the ith matched unigram in reference is content word.

$$c_r(i) = \begin{cases} 1 & if\ function\ word \\ 0 & if\ not\ function\ word \end{cases}$$

F-score can be calculate by Formula (7). β is a decimal between 0 and 1, which can balance the effect of precision and recall.

$$F\text{-}score = \frac{P \times R}{\beta \times P + (1 - \beta) \times R} \tag{7}$$

Table 2. The meanings of parameters in ENTF

Parameter	Meaning
α	the parameter in ENT
β	balance the effect of precision and recall
w_f	differentiate the effect of function word and content word
w_{exact}	match weight for match module type $exact$
w_{stem}	match weight for match module type $stem$
$w_{synonym}$	match weight for match module type $synonym$
$w_{paraphrase}$	match weight for match module type $paraphrase$

2.3   ENTF

After obtained ENT and unigram F-score, we can calculate the score of ENTF as Formula (8). Both of fluency and accuracy can be evaluated by ENTF. The system level score is the average score of all the sentence scores. The meanings of all parameters in ENTF are listed in Table 2.

$$ENTF = ENT \times F\text{-}score \tag{8}$$

3   Experiment

The experiments on both system level and sentence level are carried out. On system level, the correlations are calculated using Spearman's rank correlation coefficient ρ [18]. Kendall's rank correlation coefficient τ [9] is employed to evaluate the sentence level correlation.

3.1   Data

The data we used are WMT 2012, WMT 2013 and WMT 2014 on into English direction. The number of translation systems for each language pairs are shown in Table 3.

Table 3. The number of translation systems for each language pair on WMT 2012, WMT 2013 and WMT 2014. cs-en means Czech to English, de-en means German to English, es-en means Spanish to English, fr-en means French to English, ru-en means Russian to English, and hi-en means Hindi to English.

Language	cs-en	de-en	es-en	fr-en	ru-en	hi-en
WMT 2012	6	16	12	15	-	-
WMT 2013	12	23	17	19	23	-
WMT 2014	5	13	-	8	13	9

3.2   Parameter Values

For all of the parameters in ENTF except α, METEOR has the same meaning parameters, and the values are tuned. So we use the same parameter values as METEOR, and needn't tune them again. For α, we use the empirical value for system level and sentence level. All the parameter values are listed in Table 4.

Table 4. Parameter values in ENTF.

level	α	β	w_f	w_{exact}	w_{stem}	$w_{synonym}$	$w_{paraphrase}$
system	1.35	0.85	0.25	1.0	0.6	0.8	0.6
sentence	1.2						

3.3   System Level Correlation

In the experiments, we compare the performance of our metric with the widely-used lexicon-based metric such as BLEU[4], TER[5] and METEOR[6]. In addition,

---

[4] ftp://jaguar.ncsl.nist.gov/mt/resources/mteval-v13a.pl.

[5] http://www.cs.umd.edu/~snover/tercom.

[6] http://www.cs.cmu.edu/~alavie/METEOR/download/meteor-1.4.tgz.

Table 5. System level correlations on WMT 2012, WMT 2013 and WMT 2014. The value in bold is the best result in each column. *ave* stands for the average result of the language pairs on WMT 2012, WMT 2013 and WMT 2014. Metrics with * stands for the metric combining many kinds of metrics.

metrics	cs-en	de-en	es-en	fr-en	avg
TER	.886	.624	.916	.821	.812
BLEU	.886	.671	.874	.811	.811
METEOR	.657	.885	.951	.843	.834
SEMPOS	.940	**.920**	.940	.800	**.900**
ENTF	**.943**	.847	**.958**	**.846**	.899

(a) System level correlations on WMT 2012

metrics	cs-en	de-en	es-en	fr-en	ru-en	avg
TER	.800	.833	.825	.951	.581	.798
BLEU	.946	.851	.902	**.989**	.698	.877
METEOR	.964	.961	.979	.984	.789	.935
ENTF	**.982**	**.971**	**.979**	.984	**.842**	**.952**

(b) System level correlations on WMT 2013

metrics	cs-en	de-en	fr-en	hi-en	ru-en	avg
TER	.976	.775	.952	.618	.809	.826
BLEU	.909	.832	.952	.956	.789	.888
METEOR	.980	.927	.975	.457	.805	.829
*DISCOTK-PARTY-TUNED	.975	**.943**	**.977**	.956	**.870**	**.944**
*LAYERED	.941	.893	.973	**.976**	.854	.927
*DISCOTK-PARTY	.983	.921	.970	.862	.856	.918
*UPC-STOUT	.948	.915	.968	.898	.837	.913
VERTA-W	.934	.867	.959	.920	.848	.906
ENTF	**.991**	.905	.972	.922	.818	.922

(c) System level correlations on WMT 2014

we also give the best performance metrics for each year. In WMT 2012 and WMT 2013, the best performance metric is SEMPOS [13] and METEOR respectively. In WMT 2014, the best four performance metrics are not single metrics, and combine many kinds of metrics, such as DISCOTK-PARTY-TUNED [8], LAYERED [6], DISCOTK-PARTY [8] and UPC-STOUT [7]. For fairness, we also give the result of the single metric with the best performance VERTA-W [4] .

The system level correlations are shown in Table 5. The value in bold is the best result in each column. *ave* stands for the average result of the language pairs. ENTF is better than BLEU, TER and METEOR on average on WMT 2012, WMT 2013 and WMT 2014, which reflects that ENTF can properly evaluate different translations. Compared with the best performance metrics, ENTF is comparable with SEMPOS on average on WMT 2012, better than METEOR

Table 6. Sentence level correlations on WMT 2012, WMT 2013 and WMT 2014. The value in bold is the best result in each column. *ave* stands for the average result of the language pairs on WMT 2012, WMT 2013 and WMT 2014.

Language	cs-en	de-en	es-en	fr-en	avg
BLEU	.157	.191	.189	.210	.187
METEOR	.212	.275	.249	.251	.247
ENTF	**.212**	**.276**	**.251**	**.253**	**.248**

(a) Sentence level correlations on WMT 2012.

Language	cs-en	de-en	es-en	fr-en	ru-en	avg
BLEU	.199	.220	.259	.224	.162	.213
METEOR	**.265**	**.293**	**.324**	**.264**	.239	.277
ENTF	.259	.290	.320	.261	**.270**	**.280**

(b) Sentence level correlations on WMT 2013.

Language	cs-en	de-en	fr-en	hi-en	ru-en	avg
BLEU	.216	.259	.367	.286	.256	.277
METEOR	**.282**	**.334**	.406	.420	.329	.354
ENTF	.275	.333	**.411**	**.421**	**.332**	**.355**

(c) Sentence level correlations on WMT 2014.

on average on WMT 2013. On WMT 2014, ENTF is better than the best single metric VERTA-W on average. Compared with the combined metrics, ENTF is better than DISCOTK-PARTY and UPC-STOUT on average, and comparable with LAYERED, but still has lower performance than DISCOTK-PARTY-TUNED.

3.4 Sentence Level Correlation

On sentence level, we compare the performance of our metric with the widely-used lexicon-based metric such as BLEU[7] and METEOR[8].

The sentence level correlations on WMT 2012, WMT 2013 and WMT 2014 are shown in Table 6. The value in bold is the best result in each column. *ave* stands for the average result of the language pairs.

From the results in Table 6, ENTF is better than BLEU on every language pairs on WMT 2012, WMT 2013 and WMT 2014, and obtains comparable correlations with METEOR on average. The experiment results testify the effectiveness of our new metric.

---

[7] ftp://jaguar.ncsl.nist.gov/mt/resources/mteval-v13a.pl.

[8] http://www.cs.cmu.edu/~alavie/METEOR/download/meteor-1.4.tgz.

4   Conclusion and Future Work

In this paper, we propose an entropy-based automatic evaluation metric ENTF, which uses entropy of the matched words to reflect the fluency of the translation, and uses unigram F-score to reflect accuracy. Experiment shows that ENTF obtained state-of-the-art performance on system level. On sentence level, ENTF is comparable with METEOR.

One purpose of automatic evaluation metrics is to improve the quality of machine translation systems. So, in the future, we will use ENTF in the tuning process to improve the translation quality, such as MERT (Minimum Error Rate Training) [15].

Acknowledgements. This work is supported by National Natural Science Foundation of P. R. China under Grant Nos. 61379086, 61602284, 61602285, 61602282 and Shandong Provincial Natural Science Foundation of China under Grant No. ZR2015FQ009. Qun Liu's work is partially supported by the Science Foundation Ireland (Grant 13/RC/2106) as part of the ADAPT Centre at Dublin City University.

References

1. Chan, Y.S., Ng, H.T.: Maxsim: a maximum similarity metric for machine translation evaluation. In: Proceedings of ACL 2008: HLT, pp. 55–62 (2008)
2. Chen, B., Kuhn, R.: Amber: a modified bleu, enhanced ranking metric. In: Proceedings of the Sixth Workshop on Statistical Machine Translation, pp. 71–77. Association for Computational Linguistics, Edinburgh, Scotland, July 2011. http://www.aclweb.org/anthology/W11-2105
3. Chen, B., Kuhn, R., Foster, G.: Improving amber, an MT evaluation metric. In: Proceedings of the Seventh Workshop on Statistical Machine Translation, WMT 2012, pp. 59–63. Association for Computational Linguistics, Stroudsburg, PA, USA (2012). http://dl.acm.org/citation.cfm?id=2393015.2393021
4. Comelles, E., Atserias, J.: Verta participation in the WMT14 metrics task. In: Proceedings of the Ninth Workshop on Statistical Machine Translation, pp. 368–375. Association for Computational Linguistics, Baltimore, Maryland, USA, June 2014. http://www.aclweb.org/anthology/W14-3347
5. Doddington, G.: Automatic evaluation of machine translation quality using n-gram co-occurrence statistics. In: Proceedings of the Second International Conference on Human Language Technology Research, HLT 2002, pp. 138–145. Morgan Kaufmann Publishers Inc., San Francisco, CA, USA (2002). http://dl.acm.org/citation.cfm?id=1289189.1289273
6. Gautam, S., Bhattacharyya, P.: Layered: metric for machine translation evaluation. In: Proceedings of the Ninth Workshop on Statistical Machine Translation, pp. 387–393. Association for Computational Linguistics, Baltimore, Maryland, USA, June 2014. http://www.aclweb.org/anthology/W14-3350
7. Gonzàlez, M., Barrón-Cedeño, A., Màrquez, L.: Ipa and stout: leveraging linguistic and source-based features for machine translation evaluation. In: Proceedings of the Ninth Workshop on Statistical Machine Translation, pp. 394–401. Association for Computational Linguistics, Baltimore, Maryland, USA, June 2014. http://www.aclweb.org/anthology/W14-3351

8. Joty, S., Guzmán, F., Màrquez, L., Nakov, P.: Discotk: using discourse structure for machine translation evaluation. In: Proceedings of the Ninth Workshop on Statistical Machine Translation, pp. 402–408. Association for Computational Linguistics, Baltimore, Maryland, USA, June 2014. http://www.aclweb.org/anthology/W14-3352

9. Kendall, M.G.: A new measure of rank correlation. Biometrika **30**(1/2), 81–93 (1938)

10. Lavie, A., Agarwal, A.: Meteor: an automatic metric for MT evaluation with high levels of correlation with human judgments. In: Proceedings of the Second Workshop on Statistical Machine Translation. StatMT 2007, pp. 228–231. Association for Computational Linguistics, Stroudsburg, PA, USA (2007). http://dl.acm.org/citation.cfm?id=1626355.1626389

11. Liu, D., Gildea, D.: Syntactic features for evaluation of machine translation. J. Colloid Interface Sci. **332**(2), 291–297 (2005)

12. Lo, C.k., Wu, D.: Meant: an inexpensive, high-accuracy, semi-automatic metric for evaluating translation utility based on semantic roles. In: Proceedings of the 49th Annual Meeting of the Association for Computational Linguistics: Human Language Technologies, pp. 220–229. Association for Computational Linguistics, Portland, Oregon, USA, June 2011. http://www.aclweb.org/anthology/P11-1023

13. Macháček, M., Bojar, O.: Approximating a deep-syntactic metric for MT evaluation and tuning. In: Proceedings of the Sixth Workshop on Statistical Machine Translation, pp. 92–98. Association for Computational Linguistics (2011)

14. Mehay, D., Brew, C.: BLEUÂTRE: flattening syntactic dependencies for MT evaluation. In: Proceedings of the 11th Conference on Theoretical and Methodological Issues in Machine Translation (TMI) (2007)

15. Och, F.: Minimum error rate training in statistical machine translation. In: Proceedings of the 41st Annual Meeting on Association for Computational Linguistics, vol. 1, pp. 160–167. Association for Computational Linguistics (2003)

16. Owczarzak, K., van Genabith, J., Way, A.: Labelled dependencies in machine translation evaluation. In: Proceedings of the Second Workshop on Statistical Machine Translation, StatMT 2007, pp. 104–111. Association for Computational Linguistics, Stroudsburg, PA, USA (2007). http://dl.acm.org/citation.cfm?id=1626355.1626369

17. Papineni, K., Roukos, S., Ward, T., Zhu, W.: BLEU: a method for automatic evaluation of machine translation. In: Proceedings of the 40th annual meeting on association for computational linguistics, pp. 311–318. Association for Computational Linguistics (2002)

18. Pirie, W.: Spearman rank correlation coefficient. Encyclopedia of statistical sciences (1988)

19. Porter, M.F.: Snowball: a language for stemming algorithms (2001)

20. Shannon, C.E.: Communication theory of secrecy systems*. Bell Syst. Tech. J. **28**(4), 656–715 (1949)

21. Snover, M., Dorr, B., Schwartz, R., Micciulla, L., Makhoul, J.: A study of translation edit rate with targeted human annotation. In: Proceedings of Association For Machine Translation in the Americas, pp. 223–231 (2006)

22. Zhu, J., Yang, M., Wang, B., Li, S., Zhao, T.: All in strings: a powerful string-based automatic mt evaluation metric with multiple granularities. In: Proceedings of the 23rd International Conference on Computational Linguistics: Posters, COLING 2010, pp. 1533–1540. Association for Computational Linguistics, Stroudsburg, PA, USA (2010). http://dl.acm.org/citation.cfm?id=1944566.1944741

Translation Oriented Sentence Level Collocation Identification and Extraction

Xiaoxia Liu and Degen Huang$^{(\boxtimes)}$

Dalian University of Technology, No. 2, Linggong Road, Hi-Tech Zone,
Dalian 116024, China
liuxxivy@mail.dlut.edu.cn, huangdg@dlut.edu.cn

Abstract. The technique to identify and extract collocations in a given sentence is very important to sentence understanding, analysing and translating. So we propose a sentence level collocation identification and extraction method which follows the traditional two phase collocation extraction model. In candidate generating phase, we use the dependency parsing results directly, while in the filtering phase, we propose to use the latest model of distributional semantics - word embedding based similarity to filter the noises. For each candidate, three word embedding based similarity rankings will be obtained and accordingly to decide if it is a real collocation. The experimental results show that the proposed filtering method performs better than the traditional well-known association measures. The comparison with the baseline system shows that the proposed method can retrieve more collocations with higher precision than the baseline, which is of significance to sentence related natural language processing tasks.

Keywords: Word-embedding · Association measure · Collocation extraction · Collocation identification

1 Introduction

Collocations refer to the conventional word combinations which cannot be freely created according to the rules of syntax. Almost no natural language, no matter written or spoken, can do without the collocations. It is said most sentences include at least one collocation. And collocations are culture dependent, that is to say in different cultures or languages, collocations are different. All these features make the study of collocations an important task in the natural language, especially in cross language tasks such as translation.

In both fields of theoretical linguistics and computational linguistics, more and more scholars have been aware of the significance of collocations and carried out some researches on them. In the field of theoretical linguistics, the study focuses on the research, discovery and application of this linguistic phenomenon. In the field of computational linguistics, more attention is paid to the automatic identification or extraction of collocations. The accurate identification

© Springer Nature Singapore Pte Ltd. 2017
D.F. Wong and D. Xiong (Eds.): CWMT 2017, CCIS 787, pp. 78–89, 2017.
https://doi.org/10.1007/978-981-10-7134-8_8

and extraction of collocations have important implications for natural language processing tasks such as text generation, syntactic analysis, and machine translation.

In literature the identification and extraction of collocations are two different tasks. Collocation identification task is to annotate collocations in the corpus usually based on extraction results or existing collocation dictionary [1]. Collocation extraction task is to discover new collocations in the corpus. Almost all collocation extraction methods in literature follow a two stage model, with the first stage to find candidates, the second stage to filter the candidates. In the first stage, there are statistical and syntactic based methods. In the filtering stage, different association measures are used. There is no obvious difference between different association measures, and only one method is more suitable for the extraction of a certain type of collocations according to literature. Moreover, all the collocation extraction work so far extracts collocations from the whole corpus, and there are few researches on identifying and extracting collocations at sentence level. However, in practical applications, such as sentence understanding, syntactic analysis, and machine translation, it is necessary to identify and extract every collocation accurately in a given sentence.

Therefore, we propose a sentence level collocation identification and extraction system based on the state-of-the-art distributional semantics model - word embedding. By integrating the window size and the collocation part-of-speech information in the system, our collocation recognition system performs better than the baseline system in precision, recall and F-value.

2 Related Work

Collocations are an integral part of natural language, thus the study of collocation extraction becomes a basic and hot issue in natural language processing. There are so far many collocation extraction methods. Some are co-occurrence frequency based [2]. Some are based on mean and variance such as the early collocation extraction work by Smadja [3], which was later adapted by Sun et al. [4] to extract collocations in Chinese. Some are based on hypothesis testing, such as Pearson's chi-square test in [5], likelihood ratio in [6–8]. Still some are based on the concepts from information theory, such as mutual information and entropy. The methods based on mutual information use the correlation measure to replace co-occurrence measure. [9,10] use mutual information to filter the collocation candidates. [11] is to filter the candidates based on entropy. But no matter what method is used, co-occurrence based or hypothesis testing based or information theory based, they are in fact all based on the word frequency in the corpus.

Collocation extraction methods in literature usually follow a two-phase model, with the first phase to find candidates and the second to filter the noises. In candidate discovering phase the method is developed from window based to syntactic based in order to solve the distance problem. Dependency syntax is used in syntactic based method. One way to use this syntactic information is to use the dependency parsing results directly as the candidates. In this way only 2-gram collocations can be extracted. The other way is to transform the dependency relations into dependency syntactic tree and extract those frequent sub-trees as the candidates which include multi-grams. [12] is the first to use dependency syntax in collocation extraction, in which, the dependency triples consisting of a head, a dependency type and a modifier are regarded as candidates. Then mutual information is used to filter out dependency triples that occurred merely by coincidences. [13] also uses dependency syntax to extract certain types of collocations in which Fips (a dependency parsing tool) is used to extract phrases of certain types, such as adjective-noun, noun-noun, noun-preposition-noun, subject-verb, verb-object, verb-preposition as candidates, then log likelihood ratio is used to filter the noises, finally, the filtered collocations are recursively extended to get multi-grams. [14], which is our baseline, uses dependency trees to extract the multi-word expressions (including multi-gram collocations) by simply using statistical method to filter. This method is language independent and with no limit to distance between collocating words and to the number of collocating words. [10] uses a tree mining algorithm to extract frequent tree patterns, compute the point-wise mutual information by dividing a dependency tree pattern into two parts and use the average of the point-wise mutual information as an association for dependency tree patterns. This method can also obtain discontinuous multi-gram collocations. [15] also uses dependency parser in developing EXEC, a web-based system that can automatically extract English collocations and their Chinese-English bilingual examples from parallel corpora. [16] uses dependency parser to extract verb-noun in Japanese. [17,18] use dependency parser to extract 2-gram collocations from China English.

From the above analysis, we can find that the difference for different dependency syntax based methods lies in the different methods used in the filtering phase. Filtering methods are based on association measures, and there is a trend to integrate several different measures in one work since some studies on the comparison and integration of different measures prove that the integrated measures are better than when only one is used. For example, [5] compares and analyses the often used co-occurrence frequency, mutual information, chi-square test, t-test and log likelihood ratio in detail. [19] also compares different association measures in collocation extraction and integrates the frequency based measure with likelihood ratio, t-test, I-score and chi-square test. [20] selects 17 from 82 association measures, and uses regression analysis to integrate them in collocation extraction, which is proved to perform better than when only point-wise mutual information is used. Later, [21] integrates five association measures in their collocation filtering. [14] uses entropy, mutual information, etc. in their collocation filtering. [22,23] also integrate several different association measures to extract collocations.

Most association measures are based on frequency, but frequency cannot depict the syntactic and semantic relations between words. So no matter which association measures you choose and how you integrate them, the improvement is still limited. Word embedding, which depicts a word in low dimensional vector, is said can capture the syntactic and semantic characteristics of the word. So intuitively, to use word embedding to measure the relations between words might be a better choice. We proved the applicability of word embedding in measuring the syntagmatic relations between words and tested its effect in the collocation extraction task through a pilot study. In this study, we propose to use word embedding based association measure in our sentence level collocation extraction task. Experimental results show that our proposed method is better than traditional dependency based method. Besides, our proposed method combines the two tasks - identification and extraction into one task and can identify and extract collocations at the same time without relying on the existing collocation dictionary.

3   The Method

Dependency based collocation extraction is said to be the state-of-the-art method since it can solve the distance problem between collocating words. Both the adjacent collocations and collocations with distance can be extracted by this method. But filtering in dependency based method is based on those traditional association measures, such as the chi-square test, mutual information and log likelihood ratio value, which are in fact based on the occurrences of the words in the corpus. So no matter which association measure you choose and how you integrate those measures, the improvement in collocation extraction cannot be significant.

Word embedding, which uses low dimensional vector to indicate the word, can depict the inner syntactic and semantic meaning of the word very well. So, word embedding based method can measure the relations between words. There are two kinds of relations between words [24]. One is paradigmatic and the other is syntagmatic. Two words are in a syntagmatic relation if they co-occur more frequently than expected from chance and have different grammatical roles in the sentences in which they occur. Two words are in a paradigmatic relation if they can substitute for one another in a sentence without affecting the grammaticality or acceptability of the sentence. Collocations belong to syntagmatic relations. Word embedding based relation measuring method usually uses similarity computing. We use the default similarity computing - cosine similarity provided by python version of word2vec - module gensim [25]. Word embedding based similarity computing will discover words both in paradigmatic and syntagmatic relations simultaneously but at sentence level, where words in paradigmatic relations are much fewer than words in syntagmatic relations, so word embedding based similarity computing at sentence level discovers mainly words in syntagmatic relations. Thus, word embedding based association measure is proposed in our method.

Our word embedding based association measure method is based on rankings. Suppose the candidate is made up of two words, one is the headword W_h and the other is the collocating word W_c. For each candidate, there will be three word embedding based similarity rankings. The first ranking is the ranking of all the candidates in the sentence. The second ranking is the ranking of all the pairs that include headword W_h; and the third ranking is the ranking of word pairs that include candidate collocating word W_c. The three rankings show the association strength of the words in the candidates. The first ranking shows the association strength of the candidate among all the possible candidates in the sentence. The second ranking shows the association strength of the headword W_h with all other words in the sentence. The third ranking shows the association strength of the collocating word W_c with all other words in the sentence. If the candidate ranks in the first place in either ranking list, it means the candidate is more likely to be a real collocation. The filtering is thus based on these three rankings.

In our method, the task is to identify and extract collocations from a given sentence. The method is based on dependency syntax and word embedding. The resources and tools we need are: corpus to train word embedding, collocation part-of-speech patterns (which we get automatically from the test corpus. They are a list of part-of-speech combinations of the collocations in the test corpus), word embedding training tool, and a dependency parser. The procedures of our method are as the followings:

Preparation: train word embedding

Input: a sentence, word embedding, collocation part-of-speech patterns

Output: collocations in the input sentence

Procedures:

Step 1: Dependency parsing the input sentence;

Step 2: Choose every dependency pair as candidates, filter them according to window size and part-of-speech and then put them in the candidate list;

Step 3: Rank all the word pairs in the candidate list according to their word embedding based similarity;

Step 4: For each candidate pair, compute the similarity between each word in the candidate pair with the other words in the sentence, and rank them respectively. Till now, for each candidate pair, we have three ranks in different ranking lists;

Step 5: Filter the candidate list further according to the three rankings from steps 3 and 4 and also the lowest similarity limit;

Step 6: Output the remaining collocations.

4   Experiments and Analysis

4.1   Experimental Preparation

In our dependency and word embedding based collocation extraction method, two of the most important tools need to be considered: the dependency parsing tool and the word embedding training tool. For the first, we use Stanford CoreNLP [26]. Word embedding is trained by the python version of word2vec.

The size of the training corpus for word embedding is 43.6 MB, which is the Chinese part of a self-compiled Chinese-English bilingual parallel corpus[1] with 457,899 sentence pairs, 8,388,455 tokens and 57,979 word types that covers almost all the common words in modern Chinese.

4.2   Evaluation Method

The evaluation work is conducted from three perspectives: precision, recall and F-value.

$$P(recision) = \frac{correctly\ extracted\ collocations}{all\ extracted\ collocations}. \tag{1}$$

$$R(ecall) = \frac{correctly\ extracted\ collocations}{all\ collocations}. \tag{2}$$

$$F(-value) = \frac{P * R * 2}{P + R}. \tag{3}$$

The testing set is a set of 600 Chinese sentences with collocations are manually annotated. In annotating, we ask two linguistic experts to annotate the collocations in the testing sentences independently, only those agreed by the two are accepted. In evaluating we choose headword-driven evaluation method in which we evaluate the method by the collocations of certain headword. To be specific, only the collocations of the frequent headword "能力(ability)" (which is often used in many Chinese collocation extraction methods) are considered in the evaluation task.

We also compare the proposed method with the baseline system Varro, which is a tool-kit that extracts collocations from dependency tree-banks by looking for recurring connected sub-trees instead of sub-sequences in strings. The approach can find not only two gram collocations but also multi-gram collocations, not only adjacent collocations but also collocations with distance between collocating words. We choose Varro as baseline system because they do almost the same work as our method, and it is dependency based like the proposed method and the extraction results has recorded the source of the collocations so that we can easily relocate them in the sentence in order to be comparable with proposed method. This study, as the first step to test the practicability of the proposed method, only focuses on the two gram collocations.

4.3   Experiments to Decide the Best Ranking

In the proposed method, words with dependency relations are chosen as candidates. For each candidate of each headword, there will be three word embedding based similarity rankings. The filtering is thus based on these three rankings.

---

[1] The corpus is compiled specially for Chinese-English collocation pair extraction and the sentences are from on-line dictionaries, bilingual language learning websites, governmental websites that provide bilingual texts, etc.

Then the problem comes - what is the best ranking for deciding if a candidate is a real collocation or not? In order to get the best ranking threshold for the task empirically, we conducted a series of experiments. In the first experiment (E1 in Fig. 1), we set the threshold 0 for the rankings, that is, only if when there is one ranking that ranks first, the collocation is regarded as a real one. In the second experiment (E2 in Fig. 1), the threshold for the first ranking is set as 0, and for the latter two, 1. In the third experiment (E3 in Fig. 1), the threshold for the first ranking is set as 1, and for the latter two, 0. In the fourth experiment (E4 in Fig. 1), we set the threshold 1 for the rankings. In the fifth experiment (E5 in Fig. 1), we take the number of the candidates of a certain headword into consideration. When there is only one candidate for the headword in the sentence, the deciding of it only depends on the latter two rankings, and set as 1; and when there is more than one candidate, all the three are set as 1. Comparing the experimental results of different threshold settings, it is clear that the fifth achieves the best results. So in the following experiment, we choose the value in E5 as the best ranking threshold.

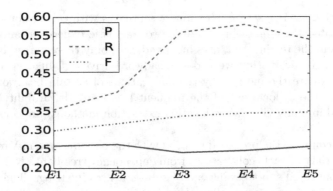

Fig. 1. Experiments for different threshold settings

4.4   Comparison Between Different Association Measures

The difference between the proposed method and the traditional dependency based methods is in the filtering phase, thus we choose well-known association measures to compare with the proposed method in order to test the applicability and effectiveness of the proposed method. The well-known association measures we choose are chi-square test, mutual information and log likelihood ratio, which are said to be the best for the collocation extraction task. The proposed method is used to filter the candidates at sentence level, but chi-square test, mutual information and log likelihood ratio based association measures are used to filter the candidates at corpus level. In order to make them comparable, we adapt those association measures to filter the collocation candidate at sentence level. In specific, we rank the candidates according to the chi-square test, mutual information and log likelihood ratio value respectively and since the proposed method chooses rank 1 as the best threshold, we choose rank 1 as the threshold for those association measures, too. That is to say, only when the candidate is ranked in the first two in the chi-square test, mutual information or log likelihood ratio based ranking, we consider the candidate as a real collocation. The comparison results are in Fig. 2.

The experimental results show that the proposed word embedding based association measure performs better in collocation extraction than those well-known three association methods especially in precision which means the proposed filtering method is competitive with the state-of-the-art methods.

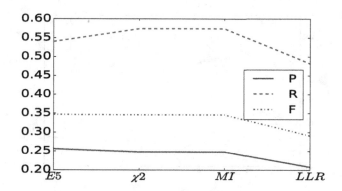

Fig. 2. Comparison with other association methods

4.5   Improvement of the Proposed Method with More Restrictive Conditions

In the proposed method, the dependency parsing results are directly used as the candidates and the similarity ranking is used to filter the candidates. On the one hand, the statistical data shows that only about 20% of dependency relations are real collocations, which means there are too many noises in the candidates. On the other hand, we think it is not sufficient by only using three similarity rankings to filter. More linguistic and non-linguistic information should be taken into consideration. Thus, we try to add several restrictive conditions in each phase of our collocation extraction system. In discovering candidates, we use window size and collocation part-of-speech patterns to filter the noisy candidates and in filtering phase we add the lowest limit to the similarity computing results since it is impossible for words with too low similarity to be in any relations. The window size we choose is 5, which is proved to be the optimal window size in window based collocation extraction [3]. The collocation part-of-speech patterns are got from the test set by collecting parts-of-speech of those annotated collocations. The lowest similarity limit is got empirically.

When adding lowest similarity limit to the filtering phase (E6 in Fig. 3) there is only a minor improvement in precision and F-value. When adding window size filtering in generating candidates (E7 in Fig. 3), the improvement in precision is significant. When adding part-of-speech filtering in generating candidates (E8 in Fig. 3), the improvements in both precision and recall are significant, thus, lead to significant improvement in F-value. Since all the three restrictive conditions can improve the method in certain ways, in the following two experiments, we integrate more than one restrictive condition in the proposed method (E9 in Fig. 3 adds two restrictive conditions in the candidate generating phase and E10 in Fig. 3 adds one in filtering phase on the basis of E9), and the experimental results show that the performance of the proposed method becomes even better.

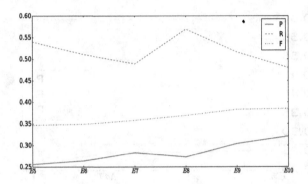

Fig. 3. Improvement of the proposed method with more restrictive conditions

4.6   Experimental Result Analysis

We compare the results of our system with the baseline Varro and find that our system is a little bit better in precision, recall and F-value than the baseline system, which means the proposed method is practicable and effective.

We conduct a comparison between the results of the two systems and find that about two thirds of the correctly extracted collocations of our system are extracted by the baseline system too and about one third are not extracted by the baseline system. This further proves that different association measures complement each other (Table 1). And a further study of this one third finds that most of them are either a verb plus a noun as the object with distance in between or a verb plus a noun with the verb functioning as a modifier of the noun or a noun plus a verb with the verb functioning as the predicate. Almost all of

Table 1. Comparison with baseline

Methods	P	R	F
Baseline	0.310	0.451	0.367
Our method	0.321	0.480	0.385

them are verb related collocations which are of significance to sentence analysis and translation. For example, collocations in the form of a verb plus a noun with the verb functioning as a modifier like 理解能力(understanding power), 预警能力 (early warning capacity), 抗震能力 (seismic resistance), 沟通能力 (communication skills), 执行能力(executive capacity) and collocations in the form of a verb plus a noun as the object with distance in between like 提高 x 能力 (improve ability), 增强 x 能力 (enforce capacity), 损害 x 能力 (damage ability), 培养 x 能力 (cultivate ability) (x represents distance) and collocations in the form of a noun plus a verb with the verb functioning as the predicate like 能力提升 (ability improved), 能力丧失 (ability lost), 能力上升 (ability improved).

Besides, even our system outperforms the baseline system, the improvement is not that significant and the precision and recall are both quite low. To find the reason for this problem, on the one hand, we carry out an analysis and find that there are 448 collocations for the headword 能力 (ability) in the testing set, but there are 1543 dependency relations which we consider as the candidates and among which only 329 are collocations. On the other hand, word embedding training corpus in our study is quite small, which may lead to incorrect similarity computing between collocating words and thus poor performance of the system.

5 Conclusion

The great difference between the proposed method and the ones in the literature is that the proposed method focuses on the identification and extraction of collocations at sentence level. Collocation identification and extraction at sentence level is very important for understanding, analysing and translating sentences. In order to extract collocations at sentence level, a word embedding based method is proposed. By using the dependency parsing results, the candidates are decided first, then, they are filtered according to the ranking results getting from word embedding based similarity computation.

Through detailed experiments, the best filtering threshold set is found out. The comparison study of the proposed method with the best association measures shows that the proposed word embedding based association measure performs better than those in the literature in collocation extraction at sentence level. The performance of the proposed method is compared with a state-of-the-art collocation extraction tool and the comparison results are that the proposed method can extract more than the baseline system with a higher precision.

The experiment results also show that the proposed system can complement the baseline system because word embedding based association measure can complement the traditional association measures. But due to small word embedding training corpus, the improvement is not that significant. So in the future, we plan to use word embedding trained from larger corpus and try to make full use of the complementary characteristic between different association measures and by integrating those best association measures in the filtering of our system to further improve the performance of our system. Further analysis also finds that dependency parsing results may be not a good choice for collocation candidate discovering, especially at sentence level, since the performance of collocation extraction system depend heavily on the dependency parsing results. Besides, not all the dependency relations are collocations. In fact, most of them (four fifths) are not. Thus, in the future, except for searching for better association measures, we also need turn our attention to researching on ways that can find candidates more effectively.

Acknowledgments. This work was supported by National Natural Science Foundation of China under Grant No. 61672127.

References

1. Silberztein, M.: INTEX: an integrated FST toolbox. In: Wood, D., Yu, S. (eds.) WIA 1997. LNCS, vol. 1436, pp. 185–197. Springer, Heidelberg (1998). https://doi.org/10.1007/BFb0031392
2. Choueka, Y., Klein, S.T., Neuwitz, E.: Automatic retrieval of frequent idiomatic and collocational expressions in a large corpus. Assoc. Lit. Linguist. Comput. J. **4**, 34–38 (1983)
3. Smadja, F.: Retrieving collocations from text: xtract. Comput. Linguist. **19**, 143–177 (1993)
4. Sun, M., Huang, C., Fang, J.: A pilot study on corpus-based quantatitive analysis of Chinese collocations. ZHONGGUOYUWEN **1**, 29–38 (1997). (in Chinese)
5. Krenn, B., Evert, S.: Can we do better than frequency? A case study on extracting PP-verb collocations. In: Proceedings of the ACL Workshop on Collocations, pp. 39–46 (2001)
6. Dunning, T.: Accurate methods for the statistics of surprise and coincidence. Comput. Linguist. **19**, 61–74 (1993)
7. Evert, S., Krenn, B.: Using Small Random Samples for the Manual Evaluation of Statistical Association Measures. Academic Press Ltd., London (2005). https://doi.org/10.1016/j.csl.2005.02.005
8. Xu, R., Lu, Q., Wong, K.F., Li, W.: Classification-based Chinese collocation extraction. In: IEEE NLP-KE 2007 - Proceedings of International Conference on National Language Processing and Knowledge Engineering, pp. 308–315 (2007). https://doi.org/10.1109/nlpke.2007.4368048
9. Church, K.W., Hanks, P.: Word association norms, mutual information, and lexicography. Comput. Linguist. **16**, 22–29 (1990). https://doi.org/10.3115/981623.981633
10. Takayama, H., Kato, Y., Ohno, T., Matsubara, S., Ishikawa, Y.: Collocation extraction using a PMI-based association measure for dependency tree pattern. In: The Tenth Symposium on Natural Language Processing, pp. 138–143 (2013)
11. Kato, Y., Kuzuhara, K., Matsubara, S.: Automatic acquisition of useful English expressions using dependency relations. In: Proceedings of Joint International Symposium on Natural Language Processing Agricultural Ontology Service, pp. 45–48 (2012)
12. Lin, D.: Automatic identification of non-compositional phrases. In: Proceedings of the 37th Annual Meeting of the Association for Computational Linguistics on Computational Linguistics, pp. 317–324. Association for Computational Linguistics (1999). https://doi.org/10.3115/1034678.1034730

13. Seretan, V., Nerima, L., Wehrli, E.: Extraction of multi-word collocations using syntactic bigram composition. In: RANLP-2003, pp. 424–431 (2003)
14. Martens, S., Vandeghinste, V.: An efficient, generic approach to extracting multi-word expressions from dependency trees. In: CoLing Workshop: Multiword Expressions: From Theory to Applications (MWE 2010), pp. 1–4 (2010)
15. Gao, Z.-M.: Automatic Identification of English Collocation Errors based on Dependency Relations. Spons. National Sci. Council. Exec. Yuan, ROC Inst. Linguist. Acad. Sin. NCCU Off. Res. Dev. 550 (2013)
16. Pereira, L., Strafella, E., Duh, K., Matsumoto, Y.: Identifying collocations using cross-lingual association measures. In: EACL 2014, p. 109 (2014). https://doi.org/10.3115/v1/w14-0819
17. Cao, J., Li, D., Huang, D.: A three-layered collocation extraction tool and its application in China English studies. In: Sun, M., Liu, Z., Zhang, M., Liu, Y. (eds.) CCL 2015. LNCS, vol. 9427, pp. 38–49. Springer, Cham (2015). https://doi.org/10.1007/978-3-319-25816-4_4
18. Li, D., Cao, J., Huang, D.: A hierachical collocation extraction tool. In: Proceedings - 2015 IEEE 5th International Conference on Big Data and Cloud Computing, BDCloud 2015, pp. 51–55. IEEE (2015). https://doi.org/10.1109/bdcloud.2015.67
19. Yang, S.: Machine learning for collocation identification. In: NLP-KE 2003, pp. 315–320 (2003). https://doi.org/10.1109/nlpke.2003.1275921
20. Pecina, P.: An extensive empirical study of collocation extraction methods. In: Proceedings of the 43rd Annual Meeting of the Association for Computational Linguistics, pp. 13–18 (2005). https://doi.org/10.3115/1628960.1628964
21. Li, W.C.: Chinese collocation extraction and its application in natural language processing. PhD. thesis. pp. 1–188 (2007)
22. Antoch, J., Prchal, L., Sarda, P.: Combining association measures for collocation extraction using clustering of receiver operating characteristic curves. J. Classif. 30, 100–123 (2013). https://doi.org/10.1007/s00357-013-9123-x
23. Dinu, A., Dinu, L.P., Sorodoc, I.T.: Aggregation methods for efficient collocation detection. In: LREC, pp. 4041–4045 (2014)
24. De Saussure, F.: Course in General Linguistics. Peter Owen, London (1915). Trans. by Baskin, W., Ed. by Bally, C., Sechehaye, A., Riedlinger, A. (1960)
25. Řehůřek, R., Sojka, P.: Software framework for topic modelling with large corpora. In: LREC 2010 Workshop on New Challenges for NLP Frameworks. pp. 45–50. Citeseer (2010)
26. Manning, C.D., Bauer, J., Finkel, J., Bethard, S.J., Surdeanu, M., McClosky, D.: The Stanford CoreNLP natural language processing toolkit. In: Proceedings of 52nd Annual Meeting of the Association for Computational Linguistics: System Demonstrations, pp. 55–60 (2014). https://doi.org/10.3115/v1/p14-5010

Combining Domain Knowledge and Deep Learning Makes NMT More Adaptive

Liang Ding, Yanqing He[(✉)], Lei Zhou, and Qingmin Liu

Institute of Scientific and Technical Information of China, Beijing 10038, China
{dingliang2015,heyq,liuqm2016}@istic.ac.cn

Abstract. In both SMT (statistical machine translation) and NMT (neural machine translation), training data often varies in source, theme and genre. It is less likely that the training data and texts in practical translation fall into a same domain, leading to a sub-optimal performance. Domain adaptation is to address such problems. Existing domain adaptive approach in machine translation employs topic model to obtain topic information. However, thus domain labels can be very much limited to in-domain and out-of-domain, when dividing topics into two types, without any more specific labels. We propose a novel domain adaptive approach to annotate Chinese sentences with CLCN (Chinese Library Classification Number) as the domain labels. We design a deep fusion model of neural network to combine two annotating models, including one applying a domain knowledge base built on thesis keywords and Chinese Scientific and Technical Vocabulary System, and the other applying deep learning method based on a CNN. Then, we have the fused domain annotator to filter the training data of NMT according to the test data. After running two predefined domain test sets on a NMT system trained by only partial of the original training data, we achieve an average 1.3 BLEU score improvement (5.4% relative), which demonstrates the feasibility and validity of proposed approach.

Keywords: NMT · Training data selection · Domain adaptation · Neural network deep fusion model

1 Introduction

As a corpus-based approach, Neural Machine Translation (NMT) [1, 2] builds up an attention-based Encoder-Decoder architecture to learn how to translate source sentences into target sentences. Its translation performance depends on many factors including translation framework, hyper parameter, the domain and the scale of training data, etc. Generally, when testing data sharing a similar domain with training data, NMT will provide a more robust translation quality. In practice, higher quality and larger scale of training data often results in its complex resources and diverse themes, which are usually different from the test data and lead to domain adaptive problems.

The goal of domain adaptation in machine translation is either filtering and devising training data, or designing and adjusting translation model, so that machine translation system can generate translation results with more domain properties. However, all the existing methods of machine translation consider test data as a benchmark and focus on

D.F. Wong and D. Xiong (Eds.): CWMT 2017, CCIS 787, pp. 90–101, 2017.
https://doi.org/10.1007/978-981-10-7134-8_9

the adjustment of training data or translation models for domain adaptation. Those methods dividing topics into two types, in-domain and out-of-domain, lack of more specific domain labels for their training data or test data. In this paper, CLCN (Chinese Library Classification Number) [3] is considered as domain labels, and two methods are used to automatically annotate the domain of Chinese sentences. Such knowledge organization information as thesis keywords and CSTVS (Chinese Scientific and Technical Vocabulary System) [4] are used to construct domain knowledge base which helps to annotate Chinese sentences' domains. This method is combined with a deep learning based domain annotating method by designing a deep fusion model of neural network to obtain more accurate domain labels. After testing NMT on two specific domain test sets, experiments show that only a part of the training data can achieve approximate 1.3 BLEU score (5.4% relative). This shows that our method lowers the training cost and reduces the unknown-word (UNK) problems. The proposed approach has a broad practical application prospect in machine translation for multi-domain scientific and technological literature, automatic construction of domain knowledge base and other natural language processing tasks.

The paper is organized as follows: after the introduction in Sect. 1, Sect. 2 gives the related work. Section 3 describes the proposed approach. Section 4 demonstrates our experiments and Sect. 5 is the conclusion and future prospects.

2 Related Work

The domain adaptive method in machine translation can be classified into four categories, data selection method, hybrid model method, semi-supervised learning method and topic model method.

By designing similarity functions the data selection method can select the training data which are similar to test data. TF-IDF in information retrieval is used to select the language model data [5, 6]. Lü et al. proposed an offline translation method to use TF-IDF to assign weight for each bilingual sentence pair in training data [7]. The above methods differs in how to design similarity functions or which data are chosen to process.

The hybrid model methods are more suitable for online machine translation, which divide training data into several parts, then use each part to train the translation sub-model and assign weights for each sub-model according to the context of test data. Koehn and Schroeder use minimum error rate training to adjust the parameters of the hybrid model [8]. Finch and Sumita train hybrid model for different types of sentences, such as interrogative sentences and declarative sentences [9]. Without considering the topic content of test data, hybrid methods focus on weights or parameters of the translation sub-model.

The semi-supervised learning method puts test sentences with its translation results into training data to re-train the translation system iteratively until the system acquires a stable performance. Ueffing and Haffari adopt semi-supervised transductive learning approach [10]. Wu et al. [11] train translation system by using the out-of-domain data, and then improve translation performance of system by adding translation dictionary and monolingual corpus in target domain. In NMT, Luong and Manning pre-train with large-scale out-of-domain data and fine tune in small-scale in-domain data [12].

Topic models establish co-occurrence matrix for words and documents to get generative model to infer the topics. The models can cluster documents according to a given topic with a certain probability, and then automatically acquire the relationship between words. Hidden Markov Models and bilingual topic model are combined to improve the accuracy of word alignment which then improves the performance of machine translation [13, 14]. Xiao et al. proposes a topic similarity model to exploit topic information at the synchronous rule level for hierarchical phrase-based translation, associates each synchronous rule with a topic distribution, and select desirable rules according to the similarity of their topic distributions with given documents [15]. Zhang et al. [16] add topic information to training data by topic model and improve the encoder-decoder framework of NMT with mixing topic information. Topic model methods consider topic information in texts, but their topics are automatically obtained in training on document sets, especially unsupervised learning algorithm. There are no explicit expressions of topic information.

Domain adaptation in NMT is relatively less than in SMT. They also did not give more specific domain labels and most of the corpus is roughly divided into in-domain and out-of-domain [17, 18]. However, the practical translation system for scientific and technical (S&T) literature often faces multi-domain texts. This paper utilizes existing knowledge organization [19–21] information to obtain more explicit domain knowledge to automatically label Chinese sentences' domain. A deep fusion model of neural network is used to combine the method and a deep learning based method [22]. Our fusion model enhances the accuracy of sentences' domain labeling and improves the quality of machine translation.

3 Deep Fusion Method of Neural Network

3.1 Construction of Domain Knowledge Base

Domain knowledge base is one form of knowledge organization and is usually constructed of words and phrases level. It is often distributed in different domains according to specific scenes or tasks. Thus, prior knowledge is well retained and helps benefit many NLP task, such as dictionary compilation, sentiment classification, machine translation and dialogue system etc.

The keywords of published thesis provided by Wanfang Data and CSTVS, are used to construct a domain knowledge base. In this paper only 4 domains in CLCN are involved, including F (*Economy-经济类*, Q (*Biological science-生物科学类*), T (*Industrial engineering-工业工程类*) and U (*Transportation-交通运输类*), hereinafter referred as F, Q, T and U.

Figure 1 demonstrates the construction process. The keywords of published thesis and CSTVS are considered as the original domain knowledge base. In order to enhance its domain expression ability, domain vocabulary from the CSTVS is mapped to CLCN classification system in this way, New Energy Automobile Chapter ⇒ U Transportation category, New Energy and Intellectual Material ⇒ T Technology.

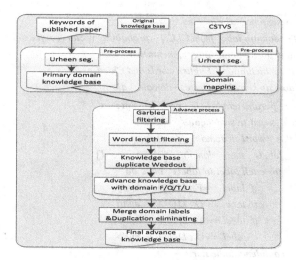

Fig. 1. Construction process of domain knowledge base

The original domain knowledge base contains a lot of terms or phrases as well as irregular characters. Such preprocess as word segmentation, garbled characters filtering, improves match rates to get a primary domain knowledge base with smaller granularity. Based on Sun et al. [23], length filtering and duplication removing is then implemented to retain words of 2–4 characters to form an advanced domain knowledge base. Some words involve multi-domains, for example, "化合物 (compound)" in "F", "Q", "T" and "U". By integrating four different domains together and removing word duplication in different domains, a whole domain knowledge base is generated and can increase the search efficiency.

3.2 Domain Labeling Based on Domain Knowledge

Figure 2 gives domain labeling algorithm based on domain knowledge. A Chinese sentence is automatically labeled with a domain based on the above domain knowledge based. Taking the 4 domain as an example, a confidence indicator and a four-dimensional probability vector are also computed. Given a Chinese sentence, after filtering punctuation, English letters and some Chinese words whose length is less than 1 character or more than 4 characters, each retained words in the sentence is checked in the domain knowledge base to get its domain label. Then the domain labeling frequency of a whole sentence is denoted sequentially as $[F, Q, T, U]$ vectors. And the frequency vector is normalized through softmax into probability vectors. The confidence indicator is assigned to the domain label with largest probability.

3.3 Domain Labeling Based on Deep Learning

Neural networks can be applied to label sentence with domain information and CNN can do classification on short texts [24]. On the basis of Kim's research, through local

INPUT: a sentence to be labeled
OUTPUT: domain label from CLCN、probability vector、confidence indicator
1: Maximum positive matching segmentation
2: Filtering punctuation、English words and Chinese words
3: Load domain knowledge base to domain _ dic
4: Initialize parameters $L, \bar{L}, L\_prob, L\_soft \max$
5: for each _ word in sentence do
6:    if this _ word in domain _ dic then
7:       labels _ tmp = domain _ dic[this _ word]
8:       for each label in labels _ tmps do
9:          if label == F : L[F]++ endif
10:         if label == Q : L[Q]++ endif
11:         if label == T : L[T]++ endif
12:         if label == U : L[U]++ endif
13:       confidence indicator ++
14:    else pass
15: endfor
16: $\bar{L} = avergae(L)$
17: for label in L do
18:    $L\_prob[label] = L[label] / \sum L$
19:    $L\_soft\max[label] = \exp(L\_prob[label]) / \sum \exp(L\_prob)$
20: endfor
21: Output max score label of L _ soft max[label] as domain result
22: Output L _ soft max as prob. vector
23: Output confidence indicator

Fig. 2. Sentence labeling algorithm based on domain knowledge

embedding, an effective end2class architecture is designed to train sentence domain annotator. Figure 3 is the deep learning network based on CNN. For more details, please refer to [22].

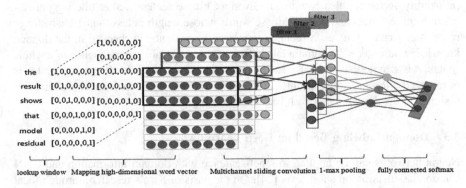

Fig. 3. Deep learning network based on CNN

3.4 Deep Fusion Model of Neural Network

The domain labeling method based on domain knowledge takes advantage of explicit and discrete domain knowledge, while deep learning based labeling method makes use of implicit and continuous semantic knowledge. So deep integration of the two classifiers may help each other and learn from each other.

In the deep fusion model of neural network, a multi-layer perceptron is designed in the top layer as Fig. 4. The results from two labelers are denoted as probability vector I and probability vector II. These two vectors can be taken as the input of the deep fusion model, including a double-layer perceptron as the top layer, and two neurons in the hidden layer to receive four-dimensional vectors. The activation function is ReLU (rectified linear Unit), and the neurons in the hidden layer can be computed as follows:

$$y_1 = \mathrm{Re}\,LU(W_1 x_1 + b_1), \quad y_2 = \mathrm{Re}\,LU(W_2 x_2 + b_2)$$

We choose ReLU for its quick convergence and set up a dropout rate as 25% to avoid overfitting. The output layer uses a softmax as:

$$y\_output = soft\mathrm{max}(W_3 y\_drop + b_3)$$

In training cross-entropy equation is used as the loss function:

$$H_{y'}(y) = -\sum_i y_i' \log(y_i)$$

where y_i is the domain label after softmax and y_i' is the right domain label. The optimizer is a self-adaptive Adagrad and the learning rate is 0.3. Batch training is run on training data.

3.5 NMT Domain Adaptation

The encoder of the NMT system is Bi-LSTM (Bidirectional Long Short Term Memory). Bi-LSTM consists of two encoding layer, one reading a forward sequence of the sentence and the other reading a backward sequence. Vectors of each sequence are concatenated. The decoding layer is also constructed based on Bi-LSTM with the same architecture. Since there are more than one layers in this encoder-decoder architecture, residual connections are applied to keep it from vanishing gradient and information loss caused by an increasing number of layers.

The domain labeling method described in 3.2–3.4 is used to filter training data of NMT according to the development data and the testing data. Firstly we get domain labels for each source Chinese sentence in the training data, development set and test set. Then we filter out sentence pairs from training data which source sentence have the same labels with the labels in the target domain label set. Thus each domain labels have different number of sentence pairs. We sort them according to the number of sentence pair and set different gradient of thresholds to select training data. All the sentence pairs in the selected training data are domain-consistent with the development set and the test set.

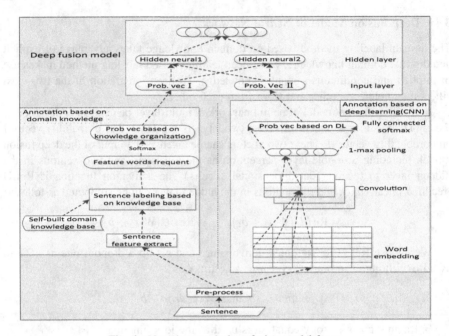

Fig. 4. Neural network deep fusion model frame

4 Experiments

The experiment firstly verifies the domain annotation performance, (here evaluation standard are the Precision rate, Recall rate and F-1 score), and then verifies the NMT domain adaptation effect (here evaluation standard is the case insensitive BLEU-4 with the shortest length penalty).

4.1 Construction of Domain Knowledge Base

Table 1 is statistic information of different domain knowledge base. Domain knowledge base causes an increase in scale from 416107 to 297632. The integrated domain knowledge base, with the size of nearly 30 million, is the final version for our experiment. Each phrase in the domain knowledge base possesses a number of labels ranging from 1 to 4. A domain knowledge base including numerous phrases with multi-domain labels indicates a weak domain feature representation. Zipf's law shows that in natural language or other similar knowledge systems, word frequency is inversely proportional to its ranking level, the product of which is constant. Table 2 shows the statistics for the domain knowledge base. This result shows that the domain label rank and the size of subordinating words satisfy the Zipf's law, and proves the domain representativeness and effectiveness of the domain knowledge base.

Table 1. Domain knowledge base statistics.

Domain knowledge bases		F	Q	T	U
Original	Phrase number	472529	239748	1422776	289427
	Average length	6.34	6.78	6.48	6.12
Primary	Phrase number	1170804	591806	3491755	700864
	Average length	2.56	2.76	2.64	2.53
Advance	Phrase number	79302	79535	191495	65775
	Average length	3.53	3.64	3.68	3.55

Table 2. Domain knowledge base tag distribution table.

Distribution	Number	Ratio
1-domain label	221249	73.70%
2-domain label	49188	16.40%
3-domain label	18772	6.30%
4-domain label	10790	3.60%

4.2 Domain Annotation Performance

The statistics of the domain annotator's CH training corpus is shown in Table 3. We randomly select 1% of the corpus as the test set for the subsequent domain annotation performance experiment, with the training set of the deep learning model selected from the rest 99%. Categories and probability vectors are obtained by simultaneously using the domain knowledge based domain annotator and the deep learning based one. We first make a simple linear fusion of these two probability vectors, and then, put these two probability vectors into a deep fusion neural model to get combined categories and probability vectors. Category with the highest probability in the probability vectors is selected as the final annotated category, and four sub-experiments are carried out using the annotated category as the statistical basis for precision rate, recall rate and F1 score. The results are shown in Table 4. We carry on analysis upon four sub-experiments. The domain knowledge based annotator do many wrong-judges due to the limited coverage of domain feature word, showing a lowest score but high efficiency. Deep learning based domain annotator only, mining hidden knowledge and continuous feature upon large training set, however, is slow in training. Also, it can't make use of prior knowledge. In simple linear fusion model, Linear proportional weighting upon probability vectors generated by the two models above, combines the explicit knowledge and the implicit knowledge. However, simple fusion can hardly rectify the majority of the wrong-judges. There is no obvious promotion. Deep fusion model of neural network carries out deep integration upon the possibility vectors with a multi-layer neural network, fully taking advantages of both two annotators. It greatly reduces the wrong-judges and the improvement is significant.

Table 3. Deep learning domain annotator's training corpus statistics.

	F	Q	T	U	Total
Sent number	900000	900000	900000	600000	3300000
Ave length	30.6	29.1	29.7	30.4	29.91

Table 4. Effect of each annotation method on label performance.

	Domain knowledge	Deep learning	Simple fusion	Deep fusion
P	0.75	0.9165	0.895	0.937
R	0.74	0.91	0.887	0.9245
F-1	0.7433	0.9131	0.8907	0.931

4.3 NMT Domain Adaptation

Table 5 is the statistics of the NMT experiment, totally 800,000 pairs in training corpus from four domains. The category and probability vectors of Chinese sentences in training data are obtained simultaneously by the domain knowledge annotator and the trained deep learning annotator. We first make a simple linear fusion of these two probability vectors, and then, put these two probability vectors into the deep fusion model of neural network to get combined category and probability vectors. Validation set (development set) is randomly selected from these four domains, totally 2000 pairs. The statistics are shown in Table 6; there are two test sets, respectively from the F economy and Q biological and each set contains 2000 pairs. The statistics are shown in Table 7. The training set, validation set, and test set are not overlapping.

Table 5. Statistics of need to be marked NMT training corpus.

NMT training corpus	F	Q	T	U	Total
CH/EN number	200000	200000	200000	200000	800000
Average CH sent len	30.1	28.9	29.9	30.1	29.9
Average EN sent len	33.7	32	33	33.3	33

Table 6. Statistics of validation set.

Validation corpus	CH	EN
Number	2000	2000

Table 7. Statistics of two domains' test sets.

		CH	EN
F	Number	2000	2000
Q	Number	2000	2000

Table 8 shows the filtrated scale of the training corpus of each annotation methods. It can be found that the scale of training corpus can be reduced by fusion model. In the case of limited size of NMT vocabulary, it can obviously reduce the UNK and ensure the correlation between the training set and test set. This method also ensure the consistency of the domain, so as to make the NMT more adaptive.

Table 8. The scale of the training corpus after filtering in different annotations.

Corpus selection methods	Training corpus		Baseline	F-adaptive	Q-adaptive
Domain knowledge annotator based	CH	Number	800000	230946	425531
		Average	29.9	30.53	30.45
	EN	Number	800000	230946	425531
		Average	33	33.26	33.25
	Proportion			**28.87%**	**53.20%**
Deep learning annotator based	CH	Number		222241	206185
		Average		30.51	30.35
	EN	Number		222241	206185
		Average		33.22	32.08
	Proportion			**27.78%**	**25.77%**
Simple fusion model	CH	Number		229885	221238
		Average		30.43	30.4
	EN	Number		229885	221238
		Average		32.25	32.18
	Proportion			**28.74%**	**27.65%**
NN deep fusion model	CH	Number		215078	214709
		Average		32.53	31.32
	EN	Number		215078	214709
		Average		34.47	33.16
	Proportion			**26.88%**	**26.84%**

We carry on NMT experiments upon a small-scale high-quality corpus filtered from previous procedure, then train different systems to score upon F and Q test set, as shown in Table 9. The domain labeling method only based on deep learning not only reduces the scale of training corpus, but also improves the average value of 0.25BLEU. The domain labeling method based on simple linear fusion model also greatly reduces the scale of training corpus, been improved by 0.1BLEU upon F test set, but showing no improvements in the domain of Q. It shows that this scheme is effective for saving training expenses and selecting training corpus, but is less likely to improve the translation quality. Finally, In the domain adapted NMT system based deep fusion neural model, the scale of training corpus is reduced to the maximum extent, and translation quality is improved on average by 1.3BLEU (relative percentage 5.4%).

Table 9. Scoring in test set for different domain adaption methods.

BLEU score	Test set	
	F	Q
Baseline	22.4	23.6
Domain knowledge based	21.9	23.1
Deep learning based	22.6	23.9
Simple fusion model	22.6	23.5
NN deep fusion model	**23.7**	**24.9**

5   Conclusion and Prospect

This paper introduces data selection method and semi-supervised learning method into machine translation for domain adaptation. First, the domain knowledge base is constructed by using the knowledge organization data such as the keywords and CSTVS. Then the architecture of deep fusion neural model is proposed by using the domain annotation algorithm to filter the training corpus in the machine translation. Experiments show that the method has the best translation effect, the largest proportion of scale reduction, and the reduction of training and decoding cost.

Future works we would like to do are: (1) Introduce the domain adaptation mechanism into the NMT architecture, design different domain vectors in the encoder and decoder, and improve the attention mechanism to complete domain adaptation. (2) Exploring methods to integrate the deep learning methods and prior knowledge, to improve the performance of the system, will be the future hot spot in natural language processing. We will try to use different ways adding domain prior knowledge to NMT to improve the translation quality in various domains.

Acknowledgments. This research work was partially supported by National Natural Science of China (61303152, 71503240, 71403257), and ISTIC Research Foundation Projects (ZD2017-4).

References

1. Luong, M.T, Pham, H., Manning, C.D.: Effective approaches to attention-based neural machine translation. arXiv preprint arXiv:1508.04025 (2015)
2. Bahdanau, D., Cho, K., Bengio, Y.: Neural machine translation by jointly learning to align and translate: arXiv preprint arXiv:1409.0473 (2014)
3. Shunian, C.: The first electronic edition of Chinese library classification. Lib. Inf. Serv. **3**, 55–60 (2002)
4. ISTIC.: Chinese Scientific & Technical Vocabulary System. Science and Technology Literature Press, Beijing (2014)
5. Eck, M., Vogel, S., Waibel, A.: Low cost portability for statistical machine translation based on n-gram coverage. In: Proceedings of Mtsummit X (2005)
6. Zhao, B., Eck, M., Vogel, S.: Language model adaptation for statistical machine translation with structured query models. In: Proceedings of 20th International Conference on Computational Linguistics, p. 411. Association for Computational Linguistics, The University of Geneva, Switzerland (2004)

7. Lü, Y., Huang, J., Liu, Q.: Improving statistical machine translation performance by training data selection and optimization. In: EMNLP-CoNLL 2007, Proceedings of 2007 Joint Conference on Empirical Methods in Natural Language Processing and Computational Natural Language Learning, 28–30 June 2007, Prague, Czech Republic, pp. 343–350 (2007)

8. Koehn, P., Schroeder, J.: Experiments in domain adaptation for statistical machine translation. In: Proceedings of 2nd, Workshop on Statistical Machine Translation, pp. 224–227. Association for Computational Linguistics, Prague (2007)

9. Finch, A., Sumita, E.: Dynamic model interpolation for statistical machine translation. In: Proceedings of 3rd Workshop on Statistical Machine Translation, pp. 208–215. Association for Computational Linguistics, Columbus (2008)

10. Ueffing, N., Haffari, G., Sarkar, A.: Semi-supervised model adaptation for statistical machine translation. Mach. Transl. **21**, 71–94 (2007)

11. Wu, H., Wang, H., Zong, C.: Domain adaptation for statistical machine translation with domain dictionary and monolingual corpora. In: Proceedings of 22nd International Conference on Computational Linguistics (Coling 2008), pp. 993–1000. COLING 2008 Organizing Committee, Manchester (2008)

12. Luong, M.-T., Manning, C. D.: Stanford neural machine translation systems for spoken language domains. In: International Workshop on Spoken Language Translation (2015)

13. Zhao, B., Xing, E.P.: BiTAM: bilingual topic admixture models for word alignment. In: Proceedings of COLING/ACL 2006 Main Conference Poster Sessions, pp. 969–976. Association for Computational Linguistics, Sydney (2006)

14. Zhao, B., Xing, E.P.: HM-BiTAM: bilingual topic exploration, word alignment, and translation. In: Advances in Neural Information Processing Systems, pp. 1689–1696. Vancouver, British Columbia (2008)

15. Xiao, X., Xiong, D., Zhang, M., et al.: A topic similarity model for hierarchical phrase-based translation. In: Proceedings of 50th Annual Meeting of the Association for Computational Linguistics: Human Language Technologies, pp. 750–758. Association for Computational Linguistics, Jeju (2012)

16. Zhang, J., Li, L., Andy, W., Liu, Q.: Topic-informed neural machine translation. In: Proceedings of 26th International Conference on Computational Linguistics: Technical Papers, pp. 1807–1817 (2016)

17. Chu, C., Dabre, R., Kurohashi, S.: An empirical comparison of domain adaptation methods for neural machine translation. In: Meeting of Association for Computational Linguistics (ACL 2017), pp. 385–391 (2017)

18. Freitag, M., Al-Onaizan, Y.: Fast domain adaptation for neural machine translation. arXiv preprint arXiv:1612.06897 (2016)

19. Ding, L., Li, Y., He, Y., Wang, X., Zhang, Y., Yao, C.: Experimental study on training data selection of SMT based on Chinese thesaurus. J. China Soc. Sci. Tech. Inf. J. **35**(8), 875–884 (2016)

20. Ding, L., Li, Y., He, Y., Liu, J.: Research on Japanese-Chinese S&T terminology translation based-on two-dimensional domain lexicalized domain knowledge. In: CWMT 2016, Urumchi, China, vol. 8, pp. 25–26 (2016)

21. He, Y., Ding, L., Li, Y.: Research on domain adaptation for SMT based on specific domain knowledge. In: Yang, M., Liu, S. (eds.) CWMT 2016. CCIS, vol. 668, pp. 43–60. Springer, Singapore (2016). https://doi.org/10.1007/978-981-10-3635-4_5

22. Ding, L., Yao, C., He, Y., et al.: Application of deep learning in statistical machine translation domain adaptation. J. Technol. Intell. Eng. **3**(3), 64–76 (2016)

23. Sun, M., Wang, H., Li, X., et al.: The guideline of constructing a wordlist of contemporary Chinese for information processing. J. Appl. Linguist. J. **2001**(4), 84–89 (2001)

24. Kalchbrenner, N., Grefenstette, E., Blunsom, P.: A convolutional neural network for modelling sentences. arXiv preprint arXiv:1404.2188 (2014)

Handling Many-To-One UNK Translation
for Neural Machine Translation

Fuxue Li[1,2（✉）], Du Quan[1], Wang Qiang[1], Xiao Tong[1], and Jingbo Zhu[1]

[1] Natural Language Processing Laboratory, Northeastern University,
Shengyang, China
lifuxue119@163.com
[2] Yingkou Institute of Technology, Yingkou, China

Abstract. Neural machine translation has achieved remarkable progress recently, but it is restricted by a limited vocabulary due to the computation complexity. All words out of the vocabulary are replaced with a single UNK, and the UNK in translation results will hurt the quality of translation. In this paper, a UNK translation method is proposed to handle the unknown word issue in neural machine translation. It uses n-best source alignment candidates for UNK translation, and can handle both word level (one-to-one) and phrase level (many-to-one) source-UNK alignment. Experiments on Chinese-to-English task shows that our method achieves a +0.73 BLEU improvement over the NMT baseline that has already employed a good UNK translation module.

Keywords: NMT · UNK Translation · Many To One

1 Introduction

Neural machine translation (NMT) models proposed in (Sutskever et al. 2014; Bahdanau et al. 2014; Cho et al. 2014; Sennrich et al. 2016) have shown promising results recently, but it has a drawback that the size of target vocabulary is limited due to the problem of high computation complexity. For example, it generally uses a small vocabulary (e.g., 50K target words) with a single "UNK" symbol. The UNK can be used to represent the translation of an out-of-vocabulary (OOV) source word. In this case, the UNK in translation results will hurt the quality of translation.

A natural way to address the UNK issue is to enlarge the size of the target vocabulary. However, it will result in high computation cost of NMT training and decoding. Recently some approaches (Luong et al. 2015a; XiaoQing and Jiajun, 2016) had been proposed to address the UNK issue in the post-processing step. The basic idea is to consider the source word with maximum attention weight as the source alignment candidate of a UNK, referred to as 1-best alignment approach, then to replace the UNK with the translation of the source alignment candidate. As the NMT attention mechanism only provides us a kind of soft alignment (Chorowski et al. 2015; Luong et al. 2015a), it cannot guarantee that

© Springer Nature Singapore Pte Ltd. 2017
D.F. Wong and D. Xiong (Eds.): CWMT 2017, CCIS 787, pp. 102–111, 2017.
https://doi.org/10.1007/978-981-10-7134-8_10

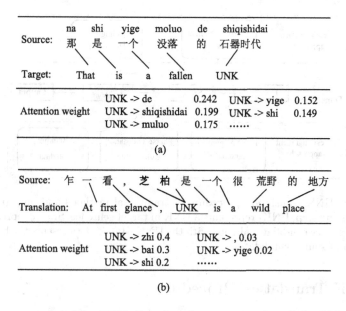

Fig. 1. Two examples of the UNK aligned to the source words and the UNK attention weight for each source word.

the 1-best source alignment indicates the most appropriate candidate for the UNK. As shown in Fig. 1(a), the 1-best source alignment candidate of the UNK is the source word "de", in fact, the UNK should be aligned to the source word "shiqishidai". In Fig. 1(b), the 1-best source alignment candidate of the UNK is the source word "zhi", actually, the UNK should be aligned to two source words "zhi bai". In other words, the 1-best alignment only handles one-to-one alignment case, and can not handle the many-to-one alignment case. Actually there are more complex alignment cases between source and target sides for two different languages, such as one-to-one, one-to-many, many-to-one alignments.

To better address the UNK issue mentioned above, this paper presents a UNK translation method that utilizes n-best source alignment candidates of the UNK instead of 1-best alignment, namely n-best alignment approach. The main contribution of this paper is that our approach focuses on both word level (one-to-one) and phrase level (many-to-one) alignment between the source words and the UNK. In addition, this approach employed on the post-processing procedure and can be used in any NMT system. In this method, a phrase-based translation rule table is used to generate the translation hypotheses of each UNK source candidate, and a language model or phrase-based forced decoding algorithm is used to choose the best translation of the UNK. Experiments on Chinese-to-English task show that our method achieves a +0.73 BLEU improvement over the NMT baseline (Fig. 2).

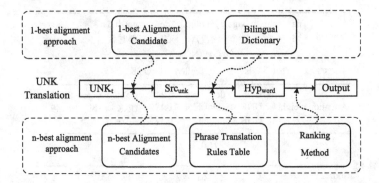

Fig. 2. The UNK translation procedure of traditional methods and our approach in post-processing step, UNK_t represents a UNK in target sentence, Src_{unk} represents corresponding source candidates aligned with the UNK, Hyp_{word} represents the hypotheses translation of source candidates

2   UNK Translation Procedure

Naturally, given a UNK in a target sentence, if we know which source word or phrase is responsible for the UNK, we could adopt the translation of corresponding source word or phrase as the UNK translation for the target sentence. Compared to the 1-best alignment approach, this paper presents n-best alignment method to obtain the alignment candidates of a UNK, and uses hypotheses ranking method to generate the final translation of the UNK. Some technical details will be introduced in the following sections. In principle, Given a UNK in the target sentence, our approach to UNK translation procedure can be demonstrated by three following steps:

Step 1: Using alignment candidate generation method to find the corresponding source words aligned with the UNK, referred to as alignment candidate generation;
Step 2: Using hypothesis selection method to generate translation hypotheses for each UNK source candidate, referred to as hypothesis selection;
Step 3: Using hypothesis ranking method to choose the best translation hypothesis of the UNK, referred to as hypothesis ranking.

2.1   Alignment Candidate Generation

As we know, the 1-best alignment approach regards the source word with the maximum attention weight as the source alignment candidate of UNK. Actually, the NMT attention mechanism only provides us a kind of soft alignment it cannot guarantee that the 1-best source alignment indicates the most appropriate candidate for the UNK. For example, in Fig. 3(a) and (b), the source alignment candidate of the UNK generated by 1-best alignment approach are not the appropriate candidate for the UNK.

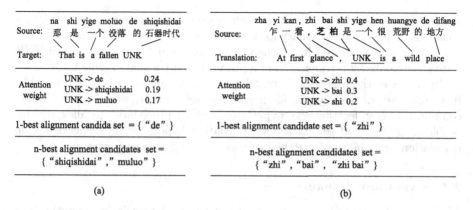

Fig. 3. Two examples of alignment candidate set generated by 1-best candidate set and n-best candidates where n is set to 3.

To address this issue, the n-best alignment approach is proposed to find the source alignment words aligned to a UNK. To be specifically, we regard the source words with the top-n maximum attention weights as the UNK source alignment candidates. Compared with the 1-best alignment approach, the n-best alignment approach has two differences substantially. First, instead of taking the source word with the maximum attention weight as the UNK alignment candidate, it considers more source words (top-n attention weights) to be the possible alignment candidates. Second, it not only focuses on word-level alignment (one-to-one), but also phrase-level alignment (many-to-one) alignment.

In the procedure of alignment candidate generation, a stopword set is introduced to generate the UNK source alignment candidate set. The source word in the stopword set should be removed from the set. The alignment candidate set of a UNK can be produced by the following four steps:

Step 1: Obtain word-level top-n source alignment candidates in terms of attention weight, and add them into the UNK alignment candidate set.
Step 2: Remove the candidates which are in the stopword set from the UNK source alignment candidate set.
Step 3: If any two candidates in this set are consecutive in the source sentence, a new phrase-level candidate composing of both two candidates will be added in this set.
Step 4: Loop Step 3 until no any new phrase level candidate can be produced.

Take the phrase level alignment candidate "zhi bai" in Fig. 3(b), it is composed of two word-level candidates "zhi" and "bai".

2.2 Hypothesis Selection

A natural way to obtain translation hypothesis of each UNK source alignment candidate is to utilize a bilingual dictionary. However, it often suffers from a limited coverage problem. And it is a time-consuming task to manually construct a large-scale bilingual dictionary for this purpose. To address this challenge, this paper presents an approach to generating translation hypothesis of each UNK source candidate by retrieving from a phrase-based translation rule table.

In practice, there are many translations for a candidate in the rule table. If we consider all translations for hypotheses selection, it would result in high computation cost for the next hypothesis ranking procedure. To alleviate this problem, out method selects top-M translation hypotheses in terms of lexical translation probability of matched rules, e.g., M = 200 in our experiments.

2.3   Hypothesis Ranking

The goal of hypothesis ranking is to select the best translation hypothesis of the UNK from its all possible translation hypotheses produced in hypothesis selection procedure. Assume that there is a UNK appearing in its target sentence produced by an existed NMT system, and there are K translation hypotheses of the UNK, in this case we can obtain K new target sentences of the give source sentence. To evaluate each translation hypothesis of the UNK, this paper proposes two approaches to rank the translation hypotheses of the UNK.

Language model (LM). To rank the translation hypotheses, we can utilize the language model which is trained by large scale monolingual corpus, and kenlm (Heafield 2011) is selected to train the language model. For all the translation hypotheses of a UNK, we can calculate their language model scores and rank them inversely, then take the translation hypothesis with the maximum model score as the final UNK translation.

In this case, all the target sentences of the same source sentence are almost same except the part of the UNK translation. In this case, it is unnecessary to calculate the model score for each whole target translation hypothesis. In other words, for the "variable parts" of the target translation, the left and the right contexts remain constant, therefore we can mainly focus on the "variable part" which is the UNK translation for each target sentence. This simple idea can speed up the procedure greatly with no negative effects on hypothesis ranking.

Phrase-based forced decoding. As we know, the language model is an important feature for typical phrase-based decoding method in statistical machine translation community, and the phrase based decoding method also considers other features to rank the hypotheses during the beam search, such as the reordering feature. Inspired by the typical phrase-based decoding method, this paper proposes phrase-based forced decoding technique (Zhu et al. 2012) to score and rank all the translation hypotheses of the UNK.

Compared with the method which utilizes language model score as evaluation criterion, the forced decoding method utilizes all the features of typical phrase-based decoding method in SMT and is expected to perform better. Besides, if there are too many translation hypotheses for a UNK, it would result in high decoding cost for hypothesis ranking. To speed up the procedure, we adopt the same method taken in language model mentioned above.

3 Experiment

In this section, some experiments are carried out on Chinese to English translation task. A NMT system with 2 layers LSTM network with attention model (Luong et al. 2015a) is constructed. The open source NiuTrans system (Xiao et al. 2012) is selected to build the SMT system.

3.1 Settings

The training set consists of 1.85 million sentence pairs1 with 39.53M Chinese words and 45.01M English words, and the maximum length of the training set and valid set are restricted to 80 words. We limit the size of source vocabulary and target vocabulary to 80k, 50k respectively. The number of hidden units is 1000 for both encoder and decoder, and the word embeddings dimension is 1000 for both source words and target words. NIST 06 was selected as the valid set, and the test set is NIST 04, 05 and 08. To train the SMT model, the base feature set used is similar to that used in (Marcu et al. 2006). To train the SMT model, the base feature set used is similar to that used in (Marcu et al. 2006). All features were combined log-linearly and their weights were estimated by performing minimum error rate training (MERT) (Och 2003).

3.2 Results

Table 1 shows the experiment results on test set NIST 04, 05 and 08. The n-best approach shows better performance than baseline. Compared with the 1-best alignment candidate method, the n-best approach improves the bleu reaches 0.25 average on the three test sets. In the n-best approach, two ranking method (LM and PD) are implemented on the valid set and three test sets. The bleu on the two ranking method show little difference. The result is not consistent with our expectations that the PD ranking method utilizes more features than LM method may perform better. The possible reason we guess is that there is risk of failure in forced decoding, and the failed sentences cannot be selected as the translation hypotheses. Due to the little difference of the two ranking methods (LM and PD), to simplify the description, we adopt the LM method in the following experiments.

Single UNK Translation. Another test is implemented on the sentences which contain a single UNK. 505 sentences which only contain a single UNK are selected from the test set mt04, mt05 and mt08, then they are evaluated by the correctness of the UNK translation manually. As shown in Table 2, 1-best alignment approach can handle 157 cases, which only reaches 31.1% on the test set, and

Table 1. Chinese-to-English translation performance (IBM-BLEU4(%))on test set NIST 04,05 and 08. NMT is the NMT model with attention mechanism which is adopted as our baseline without UNK replacement. NMT + 1-best is the traditional approach to translate the UNK. NMT + n-best + LM is our approach which ranks the hypotheses by language model. NMT + n-best + PD ranks the hypotheses by phrased-based forced decoding model score. "*" indicates significantly better on test performance at the p = 0.05 level, compared with the baseline.

Method	Description	Dev/valid set	Test set		
		Mt06	Mt04	Mt05	Mt08
SMT	PBMT	32.16	36.71	31.32	26.45
NMT	Baseline	34.72	42.10	33.43	27.87
NMT+1-best	1-best	35.13 (+0.41)	42.50 (+0.49)	33.90 (+0.47)	28.39 (+0.52)
NMT+n-best+LM	Rank hypotheses by language model	35.42 (+0.7)	42.83 (+0.73)	34.14 (+0.71)	28.64 (+0.77)
NMT+n-best+PD	Rank hypothese by forced decoding	35.40 (+0.68)	42.85 (+0.75)	34.16 (+0.73)	28.63 (+0.76)

Table 2. The performance of single UNK translation on different method. "right to wrong" represents that 1-best method translates the UNK right, but other methods translate error, "wrong to right" is in the opposite.

Method	Right	Wrong	Right to wrong	Wrong to right
1-best	157	348	-	-
1-best + stopword	205	300	12	60
-best + LM	245	260	25	113
n-best + PD	248	257	27	118

there still exists 348 UNK translation errors need to be handled. We can find that the LM ranking method and PD ranking method show little difference on the single UNK translation. Compared with the 1-best method, our methods (LM and PD) handle more than 245 cases and improve nearly 58%. The bad news is that some errors are introduced by this method.

Compared with the 1-best method, we are surprised to find that the stopword set can handle more 48 cases. It improves nearly 30% than the 1-best method although some errors are also be introduced. We find that there are still 257 UNK translation errors which account for more than fifty percent of the proportion. We analyse the UNK translation error examples, and find that the accurate UNK source alignment candidate does not exist int the alignment candidate set. In other words, both the 1-best method and n-best method utilize the attention weight to get the alignment between the UNK and source word, and the accurate alignment candidate does not exist in the source words with

Table 3. Several examples are translated by traditional and our approach

Case 1:	Chinese	研究慢性咽炎的细菌学问题 .
	Attention weights	"的 **0.24**", "细菌学 0.23", , "咽炎 0.15", "问题 0.11", ".
	Baseline	0.09"
	NMT+1-best	Study the **UNK** problem of chronic pharyngitis .
	NMT+n-best	Study the **the** problem of chronic pharyngitis .
		Study the **bacteriological** problem of chronic pharyngitis .
Case 2:	Chinese	乍一看，芝柏是一个很荒野的地方
	Attention weights	"**芝 0.4**" "柏 0.3" "是 0.2" ", 0.03" "一个 0.02"
	Baseline	At first glance, **UNK** is a wild place .
	NMT+1-best	At first glance, **cheese** is a wild place .
	NMT+n-best	At first glance, **Perregaux** is a wild place .
Case 3:	Chinese	你想过当一名新闻播音员吗?
	Attention weights	"新闻 0.35" "播音员 0.21" "一名 0.19" "当 0.11" "? 0.03"
	Baseline	Have you ever thought about being a **UNK**?
	NMT+1-best	Have you ever thought about being a **news**?
	NMT+n-best	Have you ever thought about being a **newscaster**?

top-n attention weight, both the 1-best method and the n-best method cannot choose the accurate alignment candidate for the UNK.

Table 3 shows several samples which are handled by two approaches. From the result of the three cases, it can be seen that our approach performs better than that of baseline and traditional approach. In case 1, the result of 1-best alignment candidate is incorrect because of wrong alignment: UNK to "的", while ours get the right alignment candidate and translation. In case 2, the result of 1-best alignment candidate is incorrect because of wrong alignment: UNK to "芝", while ours is perfect alignment UNK to "芝柏" and accurate translation. Case 3 is the same as case 2, the UNK should aligned to the phrase "新闻播音员", but the 1-best method make the UNK aligned to the part of phrase.

It can be seen that the approach proposed in this work could handle many-to-one alignment between source words and UNK in target translation. In other words, the proposed approach focuses on both the word-level replacement (one-to-one alignment) and the phrase-level replacement (many-toone alignment).

4   Related Work

Several approaches have been proposed towards solving the unknown words problem which could be divided into three categories. One type of these methods focuses on enlarging vocabulary without slowing the computation speed, such as the hierarchical softmax (Morin and Bengio 2005), importance sampling (Bengio and Senecal, 2008; Jean et al. 2014), but it still suffers from the unknown word problem. The second category uses information from the context, the notable work is that Luong et al. (2015b) proposed Copyable Model, PosALL Model and PosUnk Model, and used a dictionary to replace UNK in post-processing step. XiaoQing and Jiajun (2016) utilized monolingual data to construct "substitution-translationrestoration" model to handle the UNK issue. The third category of the approaches changes the unit of input and output words to a smaller unit to allievate the UNK issue, such as characters (Gers et al. 2000; Chung et al. 2016) or bytecodes (Sennrich et al. 2015; Gillick et al. 2015).

The proposed approach in post-processing procedure is different from previous work. First, the strategy to select alignment candidates of UNK is different. Luong utilizes the NMT model to emit the source alignment position of the UNK, and 1-best alignment approach uses the attention weights to get the source alignment for a given UNK, while our approach utilizes n-best alignment candidates. Second, the ways to generate UNK translation is different. All the traditional approaches utilize a dictionary and only uses one translation hypothesis. Our approach utilizes the translation rules extracted from word alignment and considers multiple translation hypotheses. Third, all the traditional approaches can only handle one-to-one alignment between source word and the UNK, ours can handle both one-to-one alignment and many-toone alignment (multiple source words aligned to one UNK).

5   Conclusion

This paper presents a UNK translation method to handle the UNK issue for NMT. Compared to traditional methods, the proposed approach utilizes n-best alignments to generate the source word candidates aligned to the UNK, and utilizes a phrase tables translation rules to generate the translation hypotheses, then ranks the translation hypotheses to get the best translation. The n-best alignment approach has an ability to handle both word-level one-to-one alignment and phrase-level many-toone alignment cases between source words and the UNK. In the future work, we will study how to effectively alleviate the UNK issue during the decoding procedure.

References

Bahdanau, D., Cho, K., Bengio, Y.: Neural machine translation by jointly learning to align and translate. arXiv preprint arXiv:1409.0473 (2014)

Bengio, Y., Senecal, J.: Adaptive importance sampling to accelerate training of a neural probabilistic language model. IEEE Trans. Neural Netw. **19**(4), 713–722 (2008)

Cho, K., Van Merri Senboer, B., Bahdanau, D., Bengio, Y.: On the properties of neural machine translation, encoder-decoder approaches. arXiv preprint arXiv:1409.1259 (2014)

Chorowski, J.K., Bahdanau, D., Serdyuk, D., Cho, K., Bengio, Y.: Attention-based models for speech recognition. In: Advances in Neural Information Processing Systems, pp. 577–585 (2015)

Chung, J., Cho, K., Bengio, Y.: A character-level decoder without explicit segmentation for neural machine translation. arXiv preprint arXiv:1603.06147 (2016)

Gers, F.A., Schmidhuber, J., Cummins, F.: Learning to forget: continual prediction with LSTM. Neural Comput. **12**(10), 2451–2471 (2000)

Gillick, D., Brunk, C., Vinyals, O., Subramanya, A.: Multilingual language processing from bytes. arXiv preprint arXiv:1512.00103 (2015)

Heafield, K.: Kenlm: faster and smaller language model queries. In: Proceedings of 6th Workshop on Statistical Machine Translation, pp. 187–197. Association for Computational Linguistics (2011)

Hochreiter, S., Schmidhuber, J.: Long short-term memory. Neural Comput. **9**(8), 1735–1780 (1997)

Jean, S., Cho, K., Memisevic, R., Bengio, Y.: On using very large target vocabulary for neural machine translation, pp. 1–10 (2014)

Koehn, P., Och, F.J., Marcu, D.: Statistical phrase-based translation, pp. 48–54 (2003)

Luong, M.-T., Pham, H., Manning, C.D.: Effective approaches to attention based neural machine translation. In: Proceedings of NAACL 2015, pp. 1412–1421 (2015a)

Luong, M.-T., Sutskever, I., Le, Q.V., Vinyals, O., Zaremba, W.: Addressing the rare word problem in neural machine translation. In: Proceedings of ACL 2015, pp. 11–19.s (2015b)

Morin, F., Bengio, Y.: Hierarchical probabilistic neural network language model. In: Aistats, vol. 5, pp. 246–252. Citeseer (2005)

Och, F.J.: Minimum error rate training in statistical machine translation, pp. 160–167 (2003)

Papineni, K., Roukos, S., Ward, T., Zhu, W.-J.: Bleu: a method for automatic evaluation of machine translation. In: Proceedings of 40th Annual Meeting on Association for Computational Linguistics, pp. 311–318. Association for Computational Linguistics (2002)

Sennrich, R., Haddow, B., Birch, A.R.: Neural machine translation of rare words with subword units, pp. 1715–1725 (2015)

Sennrich, R., Haddow, B., Birch, A.R.: Edinburgh neural machine translation systems for WMT 16. arXiv preprint arXiv:1606.02891 (2016)

Sutskever, I., Vinyals, O., Le, Q.V.: Sequence to sequence learning with neural networks. In: Advances in Neural Information Processing Systems, pp. 3104–3112 (2014)

Xiao, T., Zhu, J., Zhang, H., Li, Q.: NiuTrans: an open source toolkit for phrase based and syntax-based machine translation, pp. 19–24 (2012)

XiaoQing, L., Chengqing Z., Jiajun, Z.: Towards zero unknown word in neural machine translation (2016)

Zhu, J., Xiao, T., Zhang, C.: Learning better rule extraction with translation span alignment, pp. 280–284 (2012)

A Content-Based Neural Reordering Model for Statistical Machine Translation

Yirong Pan[1,2], Xiao Li[1,3], Yating Yang[1,3(✉)], Chenggang Mi[1,3], Rui Dong[1,3], and Wenxiao Zeng[1,3]

[1] Xinjiang Technical Institute of Physics and Chemistry, Chinese Academy of Sciences, Urumqi, China
yangyt@ms.xjb.ac.cn
[2] University of Chinese Academy of Sciences, Beijing, China
[3] Xinjiang Laboratory of Minority Speech and Language Information Processing, Urumqi, China

Abstract. Phrase-based lexicalized reordering models have attracted extensive interest in statistical machine translation (SMT) due to their capacity for dealing with swap between consecutive phrases. However, translations between two languages that with significant differences in syntactic structure have made it challenging to generate a semantically and syntactically correct word sequence. In an effort to alleviate this problem, we propose a novel content-based neural reordering model that estimates reordering probabilities based on the words of its surrounding contexts. We first utilize a simple convolutional neural network (CNN) to capture semantic contents conditioned on various sizes of context. And then we employ a softmax layer to predict the reordering orientations and probability distributions. Experimental results show that our model provides statistically obvious improvements for both Chinese-Uyghur (+0.48 on CWMT2015) and Chinese-English (+0.27 on CWMT2013) translation tasks over conventional lexicalized reordering models.

Keywords: Lexicalized reordering models · Statistical machine translation · Neural reordering model · Reordering probabilities · Semantic contents

1 Introduction

Statistical machine translation (Koehn et al. 2003; Och and Ney 2004) has been one of the most important challenges in natural language processing (NLP). In original SMT systems, reordering model was distance-based that only penalized phrase displacements proportionally to the degree of non-monotonicity without considering the issue of language dependence. Recent researches (Och et al. 2004; Koehn et al. 2007) have presented lexicalized reordering models that determine the reordering orientation of two phrases based on the phrase alignments. As lexicalized reordering models condition reordering probabilities on the words of current phrase pair and maintain a fixed reordering probability distribution for each phrase pair, they suffer from context insensitivity and content sparsity (Li et al. 2014).

© Springer Nature Singapore Pte Ltd. 2017
D.F. Wong and D. Xiong (Eds.): CWMT 2017, CCIS 787, pp. 112–123, 2017.
https://doi.org/10.1007/978-981-10-7134-8_11

In recent years, theoretical and experimental investigations have demonstrated that deep neural networks (DNNs) outperform previous methods in various NLP fields, such as speech recognition (Graves et al. 2013) and semantic classification (Liu et al. 2015). Moreover, DNNs have shown promising results in SMT reordering models, which are applied in phrase representations with RNN encoder-decoder (Cho et al. 2014), in pre-reordering model with RNN (Barone and Attardi 2015) and in dependency-based reordering model with neural classifiers (Hadiwinoto and Ng 2017). Hence, reordering models incorporating with neural networks pave a new way to improving the performance of machine translation.

Along with the line of integrating neural networks into SMT, we propose a novel content-based neural reordering model that employs pre-trained word vectors and a simple CNN model to predict reordering orientations and probability distributions. Compared with previous work (Schwenk et al. 2006; Li et al. 2014), we consider more linguistic information of words with their surrounding contexts to improve context sensitivity. And we perform probability estimation conditioned on the semantic contents of variable length contexts to reduce content sparsity. Experiments on Chinses-Uyghur (CH-UY) and Chinese-English (CH-EN) translation tasks show that our model achieves obvious improvements over lexicalized reordering models.

This paper is organized as follows: in Sect. 2, we introduce conventional lexicalized reordering models, and then the details of content-based neural reordering model are described in Sect. 3. In Sect. 4, we elaborate on experiment settings to present our model and show experimental results for two language pairs. We finally summarize our method and put forward future work.

2 Lexicalized Reordering Models

Lexicalized reordering models that estimate reordering probabilities based on the words of each phrase pair have become standard in SMT systems. They predict the reordering orientations based on the previous adjacent target phrase and apply various orientation models to measure different reordering patterns.

In general, given a source sentence $\mathbf{f}$ and a target sentence $\mathbf{e}$ that corresponds to the translation of source sentence $\mathbf{f}$, the decoder searches for the most probable translation e^* according to the following decision rule:

$$e^* = argmax\{p(e|f)\} = argmax\left\{\sum\nolimits_{j=1}^{J} \lambda_j h_j(f,e)\right\} \tag{1}$$

where $h_j(f,e)$ are J arbitrary feature functions and integrated into a log-linear framework to tune the feature weights λ_j. More formally, given a sequence of source phrases $\mathbf{f} = \{f_1, \ldots, f_p\}$, a sequence of target phrases $\mathbf{e} = \{e_1, \ldots, e_q\}$ and a phrase alignment $\mathbf{a} = \{a_1, \ldots a_n\}$ that defines the source phrase f_{a_i} for each target phrase e_i, lexicalized reordering models estimate the conditional probability of a orientation sequence $\mathbf{o} = \{o_1, \ldots o_n\}$ by the following equation:

$$p(o|f, e, a) = \prod_{i=1}^{n} p(o_i|f_{a_i}, e_i, a_{i-1}, a_i) \tag{2}$$

where each o_i takes values over the predefined orientation models. The probability is conditioned on both a_{i-1} and a_i to ensure that the orientation o_i is consistent with the phrase alignment in bilingual sentence pairs.

In our work, we mainly consider three orientation models. They are MSLR (*monotone, swap, discontinuous-left, discontinuous-right*), MSD (*monotone, swap, discontinuous*; the two discontinuous classes of MSLR orientation model are merged into one class) and Monotonicity (*monotone* or *non-monotone*; the *swap* and *discontinuous* classes of MSD orientation model are merged into *non-monotone* class). The MSD orientation model is widely used and its specific discriminant strategy is given by:

$$o_i = \begin{cases} M & \text{if } a_i - a_{i-1} = 1 \\ S & \text{if } a_i - a_{i-1} = -1 \\ D & \text{if } |a_i - a_{i-1}| \neq 1 \end{cases} \tag{3}$$

Specifically, in Monotonicity orientation model, *swap* and *discontinuous* are merged into *non-monotone* ($a_i - a_{i-1} \neq 1$) and in MSLR orientation model, *discontinuous* is divided into *discontinuous-left* ($a_i - a_{i-1} < -1$) and *discontinuous-right* ($a_i - a_{i-1} > 1$). Formally, given a phrase pair $\{f_i, e_i\}$ that derives from phrase alignments at training process, the orientation model p_o utilizes maximum likelihood estimation (MLE) to compute reordering probabilities statistically by:

$$p_o(orientation|f_i, e_i) = \frac{count(orientation, f_i, e_i)}{\sum_o count(o, f_i, e_i)} \tag{4}$$

As shown in Fig. 1, the MSD orientation models in CH-UY and CH-EN translation tasks are composed of three portions: source phrases, target phrases and reordering probabilities of current phrase pair. We observe that lexicalized reordering models maintain a fixed reordering probability distribution for each phrase pair. As the linguistic contexts and semantic contents of words are changeable, it is obviously unreasonable to employ uniform probability distributions in decoding.

```
对 外 开放 的 ||| سىرتقىراقئىئ ىچچىۋۇشىتائ اقىرارىقا سىرترىقى ||| 0.6 0.2 0.2
对 外 开放 的 伟大 ||| ىچچىۋۇشىتائ شىئ ئىقۇلۇغ ||| 0.2 0.2 0.6
对 外 开放 的 伟大 事业 ||| ىچچىۋۇشىتائ شىئ شىلرىلرىنىن ئىئ ئۇلۇغ شىلرىرىنىن ||| 0.2 0.2 0.6
对 外 开放 的 典范 ||| ىچچىۋۇشىتتىشىككك ئىئ ىسىگلۇغىسى بۇولپ ىقاىلدىك ||| 0.6 0.2 0.2
```

```
成为 普遍 共识 ||| a consensus of opinion ||| 0.6 0.2 0.2
成为 更加 ||| become even more ||| 0.2 0.2 0.6
成为 更加 重要 ||| become even more important ||| 0.2 0.2 0.6
成为 更大 ||| become an even greater ||| 0.6 0.2 0.2
```

Fig. 1. The MSD orientation models in Chinese-Uyghur and Chinese-English translation tasks. They are composed of three portions: source phrases, target phrases and reordering probabilities of current phrase pair. Lexicalized reordering models maintain a fixed reordering probability distribution for each phrase pair.

Most long phrases that contain local word reorderings only occur once in the training data. However, phrase pairs that occur in the training data for many times tend to be ambiguous because of their various reordering orientations in specific contexts and contents. Thus MLE can hardly estimate the reordering probabilities accurately.

As shown in Fig. 2, the CH-UY (written from right to left) and CH-EN phrase pairs <学习, نۆگىنىش> and <学习, learning> of MSD orientation model have various reordering orientations in different contexts and contents. It is meaningless to use fixed reordering probability distribution for each phrase pair. Therefore, we need a flexible and efficient approach to consider more contexts and identify appropriate reordering orientations.

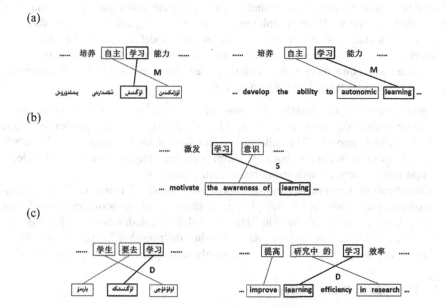

Fig. 2. Reordering ambiguity phenomena in MSD orientation models. The Chinese-Uyghur and Chinese-English phrase pairs <学习, نۆگىنىش> and <学习, learning> have various reordering orientations in different contexts and contents: (a) *monotone*, (b) *swap* and (c) *discontinuous*.

3 Content-Based Neural Reordering Model

3.1 Overview

Generally, lexicalized reorderings belong to post-processing and occur in target language, thus we estimate the reordering probability distributions based on the contents of target side contexts. Intuitively, conditioning reordering probabilities both on linguistic contexts and semantic contents will apparently alleviate phrase reordering ambiguity. Our content-based neural reordering model is given by:

$$p(o|f, e, a) = \prod_{i=1}^{n} p(o_i|f_{a_i}, e_i, a_{i-1}, a_i, c_i) \tag{5}$$

where c_i is the semantic content of variable length context in current phrase.

Taking word contexts into account will significantly enhance the ability to predict reordering orientations. As shown in Fig. 2, given a CH-UY phrase pair <学习, ئۆگىنىش>, the Uyghur grammar is subject-object-verb (SOV). On one side, when <ئۆگىنىش> is an adjective phrase and follows an adjective phrase, it should be *monotone* with its previous phrase to jointly qualify nouns. On the other side, when <ئۆگىنىش> is an object and follows a noun phrase, it should be *discontinuous* with its previous phrase because of the postpositional verb phrase. Similarly, given a CH-EN phrase pair <学习, learning>, when <learning> follows an adjective phrase <autonomic>, its reordering orientation should be *monotone* for the reason that they can integrate into a noun phrase and keep their relative position. When it follows a noun phrase especially a word <of>, its reordering orientation should be *swap*. Therefore, our model is capable of capturing the reordering orientations based on the linguistic contexts and semantic contents.

In order to acquire meaningful reordering orientations and probability distributions, we mainly consider the following two aspects:

- **Space vector representation for contexts.** Instead of using continuous space representations (Schwenk et al. 2006; Li et al. 2014), we utilize pre-trained word vectors and a simple CNN architecture to simplify the model complexity. The CNN model extracts semantic contents from variable length contexts and selects important features for reordering orientation prediction.
- **Classification for reordering orientations.** Instead of using fixed reordering probability distributions for each phrase, we build neural reordering classifier for all the extracted phrases (Xiong et al. 2006; Li et al. 2014; Hadiwinoto and Ng 2017) to predict reordering orientations and probability distributions by adding a softmax layer. And we utilize original orientation labels to optimize overall parameters.

3.2   Pre-trained Word Vectors

Initializing word vectors with pre-trained neural language model is widely employed to improve performance in the absence of a large supervised training set (Socher et al. 2011; Kim 2014). In our work, we use the publicly available *fastText* vectors of Uyghur and English that trained on Wikipedia data. These vectors have dimensionality of 300 and were obtained by using the skip-gram model (Bojanowski et al. 2016) with default parameters. In this model, each word is represented as a bag of character n-grams and the vector representation is associated to each character n-gram.

The model considers more affix information for morphologically rich languages with large vocabularies and refers to effective learning of many rare words. It is especially suitable for dealing with relevant issues of Uyghur. Moreover, it obtains representation of out-of-vocabulary (OOV) words by summing the representations of character n-grams. Therefore, we can alleviate unknown words in training process for Uyghur and English.

3.3   Space Vector Representation for Contexts

To capture semantic content of variable length context, we follow Kim (2014) to use a CNN model with one layer of convolution. Firstly, use $x_i \in \mathbb{R}^k$ as the k-dimensional word vector that corresponds to i-th word in a context. A context that contains n words can be represented as:

$$x_{1:n} = x_1 \oplus x_2 \oplus \ldots \oplus x_n \qquad (6)$$

where $\oplus$ is a concatenation operator of word vectors. The convolutional operation refers a filter $w \in \mathbb{R}^{hk}$ that corresponding to a specific window size to produce a new feature. For example, a feature f_i is generated from a window of h words $x_{i:i+h-1}$ by:

$$f_i = g(w \cdot x_{i:i+h-1} + b) \qquad (7)$$

where g is a non-linear function and $b \in \mathbb{R}$ is a bias term. One filter generates one feature and the CNN model uses multiple filters with various window sizes to obtain a feature map. Secondly, apply a max pooling operation over the feature map to extract the most important feature. Thirdly, employ random dropout on these features for regularization. Finally, all the unmasked units form the penultimate layer and are passed to a fully connected softmax layer to predict the probability distribution.

Taking phrase reordering as classification task, we propose a content-based neural reordering model to predict reordering probabilities. The neural reordering classifier takes the word contexts as input that derived from the pre-trained word vectors. The CNN model mainly consists of a convolution layer and a softmax layer. The convolution layer is used to capture the semantic contents of variable-length contexts. The softmax layer predicts the reordering orientations and probability distributions.

Formally, given the phrase pair $<f_i, e_i>$, target phrase $e_i = \{word_1, \ldots, word_n\}$ and orientation o_i, the reordering probabilities are given by:

$$p(o_i | f_i, e_i, a_{i-1}, a_i, c_i) = softmax(W \cdot C_i(word_1, \ldots, word_n) + b) \qquad (8)$$

where W is a weight matrix, $C_i(word_1, \ldots, word_n)$ is the concatenation of word vectors and b is a bias vector. To keep the comparison fair, we replace lexicalized reordering models in Moses system (Koehn et al. 2007) with our content-based neural reordering models while sharing all the other conventional features (i.e. phrase translation table, n-gram language model and beam search decoder).

3.4   Data Sampling

Using pre-trained word vectors and CNN architecture to transform the word contexts into space vectors, we can predict reasonable probability distributions. As shown in Table 1, in MSD orientation model, the orientation classes are unevenly distributed. It is inadvisable to utilize imbalance training data to predict the overall reordering probabilities based on CNN (Hensman 2015). Therefore, we employ random under-sampling method to select training examples. The aim is to ensure the proportionality of all orientation patterns and guarantee the effectiveness of our model.

Table 1. Orientation distributions in MSD orientation model

Bilingual pair	Reordering table scale	Orientation	Size	Proportion
Chinese-Uyghur	4,934,572	Monotone	3,849,728	78.0%
		Swap	173,019	3.5%
		Discontinuous	911,825	18.5%
Chinese-English	5,968,141	Monotone	3,138,851	52.6%
		Swap	477,557	8.0%
		Discontinuous	2,351,733	39.4%

Phrases that have comparability in contexts and contents should have the same orientation pattern with respective reordering probabilities. In Table 2, we list some phrase pairs that belong to different orientation classes in two language pairs.

Table 2. Reordering probability distributions in two language pairs

Bilingual Pair	Source Phrase	Target Phrase	Probability Distributions			Orientation
Chinese-Uyghur	全 国 优秀	مۇنەۋۋەر بويىچە مەملىكەت	0.718	0.003	0.279	Monotone
	打心 底 信服 法律	تولۇق قايىل قىلدۇرىشىمىز	0.048	0.705	0.247	Swap
	走 基层 看 成效	ئاساسى قاتلامغا بويرىپ	0.467	0.013	0.520	Discontinuous
Chinese-English	而是 一场 复杂	but is a complex	0.517	0.037	0.446	Monotone
	十五 计划 的 实施	for executing the 15th year	0.147	0.541	0.312	Swap
	从 骨子里 渗透	has shown from inside	0.342	0.193	0.465	Discontinuous

3.5 Training

In our experiment, the pre-trained word vectors are fine-tuned for each classification tasks. All examples of phrase pairs are extracted according to the phrase extract algorithm (Och and Ney 2004) that with maximum phrase length set to 8 words, thus we pad all the variable length phrases to the same length of 8.

Following Kim (2014), we use filter window size of 3, 4, 5 with 100 feature maps each, dropout rate of 0.5, mini-batch size of 50 and epoch of 100. Training data are randomly shuffled in the beginning of each epoch and then fed into mini-batches in order. We also use classification loss to measure the accuracy of neural reordering classifier and employ average categorical cross-entropy as objective function to compute the errors of all the training examples. Training is done through stochastic gradient descent (SGD) and backpropagation algorithm (Rumelhart et al. 1985) over shuffled mini-batches with the Adadelta update rule (Zeiler 2012) that dynamically adapts learning rate over time according to history to optimize the parameters.

3.6 Reordering Model Reconstruction Strategy

As the issue about non-separability problem mentioned in Li et al. (2014), our model is easily affected by the unaligned words, which will make great difference in determining the orientation classes of its surrounding phrases.

As shown in Fig. 3, two phrase pairs <家园, ﺍﻟﻨﺎ> and <王国, kingdom> that with various word alignments have different reordering orientations. Therefore, training examples are prone to be mixed with each other in the vector space.

Fig. 3. The non-separability problems of MSD neural reordering model in translation tasks.

We compare the neural reordering probabilities with original lexicalized reordering probabilities and maintain all the bilingual phrase pairs. In terms of the same orientation pattern with various probability distributions, we select the corresponding reordering rules in neural reordering model; otherwise the reordering rules in lexicalized reordering model will be chosen. By means of integrating two reordering models, we can maintain all the reordering examples and keep the original orientation distribution to some extent.

4 Experiments

4.1 Data Preparation

In our research, we use two publicly available datasets in CWMT. The datasets are divided into training set, development set and test set. We evaluate our content-based neural reordering model on CH-UY (CWMT 2015) and CH-EN (CWMT 2013) translation tasks. Table 3 shows the statistics of experimental data.

Table 3. The statistics of experimental data

Bilingual language	Training	Development	Test	Vocabulary	Pre-trained word vectors
Chinese-Uyghur	109,700	1,095	1,000	92,167	105,908
Chinese-English	96,000	2,000	2,000	30,126	34,820

For preprocessing, all words are converted into lowercase and tokenized by Natural Language Toolkit (NLTK; Loper and Bird 2002). Moreover, we use GIZA++ (Och and Ney 2000) as an initial step to word-aligning the parallel corpora and employ "grow-diag-final-and" strategy to establish word alignments based on the GIZA++ alignments. The 3-gram language model is trained on the monolingual training data of target language by using SRILM (Stolcke 2002). Besides, we take case-insensitive BLEU (Papineni et al. 2002) as evaluation metric and utilize *multi-bleu.perl* script to measure it.

4.2   Experiment Setup

We evaluate our content-based neural reordering models on various conventional lexicalized reordering models.

- **Distance-based:** Distance-based reordering model. The default reordering model in Moses system that penalizes phrase displacements only in terms of the degree of movements. It does not generate reordering model.
- **Monotonicity:** Monotonicity lexicalized reordering model that considers whether the current phrase pair keep the original relative position with its previous phrase pair or not (*monotone* or *non-monotone*).
- **MSD:** MSD lexicalized reordering model that considers three reordering orientations (*monotone*, *swap* and *discontinuous*) of the current phrase pair with its previous phrase pair.
- **MSLR:** MSLR lexicalized reordering model that considers four reordering orientations (*monotone*, *swap*, *discontinuous-left* and *discontinuous-right*) of the current phrase pair with its previous phrase pair.
- **Monotonicity + Neural:** Monotonicity neural reordering model that incorporates with Monotonicity lexicalized reordering model.
- **MSD + Neural:** MSD neural reordering model that incorporates with MSD lexicalized reordering model.
- **MSLR + Neural:** MSLR neural reordering model that incorporates with MSLR lexicalized reordering model.

4.3   Main Results and Discussion

Experimental results of our content-based neural reordering models against other lexicalized reordering models are listed in Table 4. We compare three types of reordering models in our experiments: distance-based model, phrase-based lexicalized model and phrase-based neural model.

As shown in Table 4, it appears that our models provide prominent gains over all other reordering models. We find that lexicalized reordering models have great advantages over distance-based reordering model, which indicates that conditioning reordering probabilities on the words of current phrase pair can improve the performance of machine translation. In Table 4, Gains on Test refers to BLEU gains on the test dataset compared with baseline models. As for lexicalized reordering models, its baseline is distance-based reordering model while it is the baseline of content-based neural reordering models simultaneously. In both translation tasks, neural reordering model that integrates with Monotonicity lexicalized reordering model provides the highest BLEU point gains; meanwhile it achieves the best BLEU score combining with MSLR lexicalized reordering model.

Seeing from Table 1, since most reordering examples belong to *monotone* orientation in CH-UY (78.0%) and CH-EN (52.6%) translation task, it is reasonable to analyze the experimental results based on orientation distributions. The Monotonicity lexicalized reordering model is equivalent to merge *swap* and *discontinuous* into *non-monotone* from MSD lexicalized reordering model, thus Monotonicity neural reordering model that adopts relative balanced orientation distributions and enough

Table 4. Experimental results of different reordering models

Bilingual language	Orientation model	Test	Development	Gains on test
Chinese-Uyghur	Distance-based	29.44	20.40	N/A
	Monotonicity	29.60	20.75	0.16
	MSD	29.86	20.74	0.42
	MSLR	29.97	20.80	*0.53*
	Monotonicity + Neural	30.08	20.92	*0.48*
	MSD + Neural	30.05	*20.94*	0.19
	MSLR + Neural	*30.26*	20.86	0.29
Chinese-English	Distance-based	20.21	18.01	N/A
	Monotonicity	20.48	18.20	0.27
	MSD	20.56	18.22	0.35
	MSLR	20.73	18.41	*0.52*
	Monotonicity + Neural	20.75	18.36	*0.27*
	MSD + Neural	20.78	18.33	0.22
	MSLR + Neural	*20.92*	*18.50*	0.19

training data can achieve obvious BLEU gains for CH-UY (+0.48) and CH-EN (+0.27). Compared with Monotonicity and MSD lexicalized reordering model, the MSLR lexicalized reordering model contains an adequate set of orientation patterns and it benefits more from the distinction of orientations between *left-discontinuous* and *right-discontinuous* for CH-UY (+0.53) and CH-EN (+0.52). In addition, we note that both the MSD and MSLR neural reordering model are overall less effective than Monotonicity neural reordering model in BLEU improvement for both translation tasks. This is probably due to the fact that there is less probability mass in CH-UY (3.5%) and CH-EN (8.0%) assigned to the *swap* category, and thus it is less helpful to employ neural reordering approach for reordering pattern analysis. Moreover, we observe that the performance of our model in CH-UY outperforms that in CH-EN. In our case, the probable explanation is that CH-UY translation is benefit a lot from the morphological word vectors that consider rich affix information for Uyghur words and alleviate the OOV problem.

In summary, our models are the most effective approaches on the two datasets: their best performances on test set and development set are 30.26 and 20.94 respectively in CH-UY translation task. The best lexicalized reordering models obtain only 29.97 and 20.80 respectively for the same sets.

5   Conclusions and Future Work

In this paper, we propose a content-based neural reordering model that applies the pre-trained word vectors and CNN model to condition the reordering probabilities on the semantic content of variable length context. This model incorporates with lexicalized reordering model to improve the ability of reordering orientation prediction. We provide experimental evidence that our model provides significant improvements for CWMT datasets and for two language pairs.

In future work, we plan to use other toolkits to align parallel corpora and extract phrases from corresponding alignments, which could alleviate the problem of non-separability and improve the accuracy of reordering feature extraction. We also plan to experiment with discriminative approach to treat our content-based neural reordering model as an additional feature and incorporate it into log-linear framework. Both statistical machine translation and neural machine translation have their merits, so it is a promising research direction to advance translation quality by combining the characteristics of them.

Acknowledgements. This research is supported by the West Light Foundation of Chinese Academy of Sciences (No. YBXM-2014-04), the Important Project on Science and Technology of Xinjiang Province (No. 2016A03007-3), the Xinjiang Province Open Project of Key Laboratory (No. 2015KL031) and the Natural Science Foundation of Xinjiang Province (No. 2015211B034).

References

Koehn, P., Och, F.J., Marcu, D.: Statistical phrase-based translation. In: Proceedings of the 2003 Conference of the North American Chapter of the Association for Computational Linguistics on Human Language Technology, vol. 1, pp. 48–54. Association for Computational Linguistics (2003)

Och, F.J., Ney, H.: The alignment template approach to statistical machine translation. Comput. Linguist. **30**(4), 417–449 (2004)

Och, F.J., Gildea, D., Khudanpur, S., et al.: A smorgasbord of features for statistical machine translation. In: Proceedings of the Human Language Technology Conference of the North American Chapter of the Association for Computational Linguistics: HLT-NAACL 2004 (2004)

Koehn, P., Hoang, H., Birch, A., et al.: Moses: open source toolkit for statistical machine translation. In: Proceedings of the 45th Annual Meeting of the ACL on Interactive Poster and Demonstration Sessions, pp. 177–180. Association for Computational Linguistics (2007)

Li, P., Liu, Y., Sun, M., et al.: A neural reordering model for phrase-based translation. In: COLING, pp. 1897–1907 (2014)

Graves, A., Mohamed, A., Hinton, G.: Speech recognition with deep recurrent neural networks. In: 2013 IEEE International Conference on Acoustics, Speech and Signal Processing (ICASSP), pp. 6645–6649. IEEE (2013)

Liu, X., Gao, J., He, X., et al.: Representation learning using multi-task deep neural networks for semantic classification and information retrieval. In: HLT-NAACL, pp. 912–921 (2015)

Cho, K., Merrienboer, B.V., Gulcehre, C., et al.: Learning phrase representations using RNN encoder-decoder for statistical machine translation. Comput. Sci. (2014)

Barone, A.V.M., Attardi, G.: Non-projective dependency-based pre-reordering with recurrent neural network for machine translation. In: Proceedings of the 53rd Annual Meeting of the Association for Computational Linguistics and the 7th International Joint Conference on Natural Language Processing, Long Papers, vol. 1, pp. 846–856 (2015)

Hadiwinoto, C., Ng, H.T.: A dependency-based neural reordering model for statistical machine translation. In: AAAI, pp. 109–115 (2017)

Schwenk, H., Dchelotte, D., Gauvain, J.L.: Continuous space language models for statistical machine translation. In: COLING/ACL on Main Conference Poster Sessions, pp. 723–730. Association for Computational Linguistics (2006)

Xiong, D., Liu, Q., Lin, S.: Maximum entropy based phrase reordering model for statistical machine translation. In: Proceedings of the 21st International Conference on Computational Linguistics and the 44th Annual Meeting of the Association for Computational Linguistics, pp. 521–528. Association for Computational Linguistics (2006)

Socher, R., Pennington, J., Huang, E.H., et al.: Semi-supervised recursive autoencoders for predicting sentiment distributions. In: Proceedings of the Conference on Empirical Methods in Natural Language Processing, pp. 151–161. Association for Computational Linguistics (2011)

Kim, Y.: Convolutional neural networks for sentence classification. arXiv preprint arXiv:1408. 5882 (2014)

Bojanowski, P., Grave, E., Joulin, A., et al.: Enriching word vectors with subword information. arXiv preprint arXiv:1607.04606 (2016)

Hensman, P., Masko, D.: The impact of imbalanced training data for convolutional neural networks. Degree Project in Computer Science, KTH Royal Institute of Technology (2015)

Rumelhart, D.E., Hinton, G.E., Williams, R.J.: Learning internal representations by error propagation (1985)

Zeiler, M.D.: ADADELTA: an adaptive learning rate method. arXiv preprint arXiv:1212.5701 (2012)

Loper, E., Bird, S.: NLTK: the natural language toolkit. In: ACL 2002 Workshop on Effective TOOLS and Methodologies for Teaching Natural Language Processing and Computational Linguistics, pp. 63–70. Association for Computational Linguistics (2002)

Och, F.J., Ney, H.: GIZA++: training of statistical translation models (2000)

Stolcke, A.: SRILM-an extensible language modeling toolkit. In: Interspeech 2002, vol. 2002 (2002)

Papineni, K., Roukos, S., Ward, T., et al.: BLEU: a method for automatic evaluation of machine translation. In: Meeting on Association for Computational Linguistics, pp. 311–318. Association for Computational Linguistics (2002)

Author Index

Printed in the United States
By Bookmasters